THE RECYCLER'S HANDBOOK

The Earth•Works Group

EarthWorks Press
Berkeley, California

For Jesse's generation. We're trying, Jess.

Created and packaged by Javnarama
Designed by Javnarama

ISBN 0-929634-08-X
First Edition 10 9 8 7 6 5 4 3 2 1

We've provided a great deal of information about
practices and products in this book. In most cases,
we've relied on advice, recommendations and research by
others whose judgments we consider accurate and free
from bias. However, we can't and don't guarantee
the results. This book offers you a start. The
responsibility for using it ultimately rests with you.

Bulk sales and premium editions are available.
For information, contact: EarthWorks Press, 1400 Shattuck
Avenue #25, Berkeley, CA 94709. (415) 841-5866.

ABOUT THE PAPER
The text of this book is printed on 8% "post-consumer"
recycled paper. However, the cover isn't printed on recycled
stock. We (and our printer) tried for several months to
find adequate recycled paper for it, and couldn't—a frustrating
and disappointing experience. We're still looking; if you know
of a source, please drop us a line. In the meantime, we
encourage more publishers to insist on recycled stock, and
hope that the paper industry will respond to our concerns.
We'll keep you posted.

ACKNOWLEDGMENTS

The EarthWorks Group would like to thank everyone who
worked with us to make this book possible, including:

- John Javna
- Catherine Dee
- Patty Glikbarg
- Fritz Springmeyer
- Michele Montez
- Steve Lautze
- Christopher Williams
- Steve Apotheker, *Resource Recycling* Magazine
- Joel Plagenz, Richard Denison, John Ruston, of EDF
- Robin Kipke Alkire
- Lyn Speakman
- Gil Friend
- Portia Sinnot
- Susan Fassberg
- Mike Goldberger
- Phil Catalfo
- Lenna Lebovich
- Fawn Smiley
- 5th St. Computer Services
- Jay Nitschke
- Jack Mingo
- Nenelle Bunnin
- John Dollison
- Richard Pruitt
- Tania Lipshutz
- Adam Davis
- Chris Calwell, Natural Resources Defense Council
- Gordon Javna
- Neil Seldman, Institute for Local Self-Reliance
- Lorrie Bodger
- Andy Sohn
- Julie Bennett
- Gretchen Brewer
- Dick Gamble
- The Ecology Center
- Susan Kattchee
- Kathleen Sinnot
- Jerry Goldstein, *Biocycle*
- S.F. Recycling Program
- David Hurd
- Debra Lynn Dadd
- *Garbage* Magazine

- Bailey Condrey, Council for Solid Waste Solutions
- Jerry Johnson, Polystyrene Packaging Council
- Chaz Miller, Glass Packaging Institute
- Carolyn Born, Moe Wright of Goodwill
- Rod Edwards, David Stuck
- The American Paper Institute
- Greg Crawford, Steel Can Recycling Institute
- John Lamb, Ron Williams of Council on Plastics Packaging and the Environment
- Elizabeth Eckl, CEIP Fund
- Evelyn Haught, Bob Garino of the Institute of Scrap Recycling Industries
- Lynne Michele, Plastics Again
- American Iron and Steel Institute
- Michael Litchfield
- Anne Scheinberg
- Liz McCormick
- Evergreen Oil
- Dana Duxbury, Waste Watch Center
- The Salvation Army
- Steve Drobinsky
- The Aluminum Association
- Steve Levitin
- Joel Makower
- Roy Gottesman, Vinyl Institute
- Bob Besso
- Textile Manufacturer's Association
- Nancy Skinner, Beth Weinberger of Local Solutions to Global Pollution
- Heinz Dinter
- Dan Knapp, Urban Ore
- Christine Donovan
- Jesse Javna
- Zena Polan, American Apparel
- Wayne Pearson, Plastics Recycling Foundation
- Dennis Kuhfus
- Butch Ries, Southwestern Bell
- Dennis Wegman, Manmade Fibers Association
- Californians Against Waste
- Pam Ottati
- Worldwatch Institute

CONTENTS

INTRODUCTION

T he success of *50 Simple Things You Can Do To Save The Earth* proved to us that people really want to do what they can to help protect the planet.

It also gave us the opportunity to find out how they want to do it ...because we've received a flood of letters since it was first published.

What have people been saying?

About half of our mail is related to recycling; so it's clear to us that Americans are genuinely interested in making it a part of their lives.

But there's a long way to go; many of the questions we're asked are extraordinarily basic, like: "Can you recycle magazines?" or "What should I do with the caps when I recycle bottles?" It's surprising that people don't have access to this information. Clearly, if recycling is going to become a part of daily life, we need to know more than we do now.

That's why we wrote *The Recycler's Handbook*. We know it's important for people to have a place to start when they're ready to get involved (or more involved) with recycling.

And *50 Simple Things* taught us that one of the most important contributions the EarthWorks Group can make is to provide information that helps individuals understand how their actions can make a difference.

Our society conditions us to believe that each of us is insignificant. It's simply not true. When we understand that, we've begun to take control of our lives...and our future.

We're at a crossroads. We can no longer afford to treat the Earth, and its resources, as if they were disposable. Recycling is a fundamental way of affirming this. Literally, we save parts of the planet...but the real power comes from our commitment to cherish and protect our home, now and in the years to come.

—John Javna, October 22, 1990

A FEW RANDOM NOTES:

• In this project, we worked closely with many people in the recycling field. We owe them a debt of gratitude. Most Americans don't know it, but these folks constitute a subculture of passionately committed individuals who have kept recycling alive for the past 20 years.

• Although they were enthusiastic, many of them had a few reservations about a book of this nature, which we feel we should pass on to you:

1. It's extraordinarily hard to write a national book about recycling, because practices are regionalized at this stage. What's true about used motor oil in California may not be pertinent in South Carolina. And in areas where there's curbside pickup, the issues are very different than those a person might face when the nearest recycling center is 20 miles away.

• With our experts' guidance, we solved that by staying general wherever it was necessary. That's why you'll see so many "Check with your local recycler"s in this book. We're not avoiding the issue—just recognizing that rules and practices may vary in different places.

2. Things are changing so fast in recycling that what's new today...or even tomorrow...could be obsolete next week. Our advice: keep checking. With any luck, the unrecyclables of today will be the recycling bonanzas of tomorrow.

3. Recyclers were concerned we'd leave things out. They were right; we have. This isn't the definitive work on recycling—that hasn't been written yet. But we have included the items and materials our experts felt were essential. And we think it's a pretty representative batch.

4. Finally, recyclers wanted to be sure you understood that if your government isn't providing the services you want, you can demand them. It may be the only way to get them, and after all, it's your right....as well as the right of future generations.

THE TRASH
MAN COMETH

Random notes from the EarthWorks Group's resident pop historian.

I n my neighborhood, Thursday is garbage day. On Wednesday night I wheel our trash can out to the curb…if I remember.

If not, I inevitably wake up at 6:30 A.M. to the whining sound of a garbage truck down the block. I throw on some clothes, dash out to the driveway, and—with a sigh of relief—hand the can over to the trash collector. The garbage disappears into his truck and I'm off the hook for another week. Like most Americans, I've rarely given much thought to where garbage goes, or what happens when it gets there. I just wanted it out of my house.

FACING THE GARBAGE

Okay, I've always managed to get it out of my house. But it turns out that just feeding the garbage truck doesn't make it disappear. We can try to hide it in a landfill or burn it in an incinerator, but with landfills overflowing and concern about air pollution growing, these disposal methods just don't cut it anymore.

That's where recycling comes in. It's more than just taking cans and bottles to a recycling center—its a fundamental change in the way we deal with garbage.

Which leads to an interesting question: How *have* we been dealing with garbage? If we understand a little about it, we're sure to appreciate what a difference recycling can make.

KEEP ON TRUCKING

The truck that picks up trash at your house every week is part of an enormous national fleet that burns millions of gallons of gas and spews out millions of tons of pollutants.

• There are an estimated 66,000 garbage trucks operating in the U.S. today. Experts say that one of every six U.S. trucks is a garbage truck.

• Garbage trucks make 500 or more stops per day, unloading several

An estimated 2 to 3 billion tires are currently stockpiled in the U.S.

times in an eight-hour period.
- The trucks only get 6 miles per gallon.
- Each holds the equivalent of 250 households' worth of garbage.

WHERE DOES THE GARBAGE GO?

Once the truck picks up your trash, it goes to one of these destinations:
- A *landfill*. 80% of all garbage generated in the U.S. is buried in landfills. But they're closing permanently at the rate of two per day.
- An *incinerator*. Since there's less and less landfill space, communities are burning more garbage at these high-tech furnaces. Only about 10% of municipal refuse is now burned, but according to one source, " 210 additional plants are planned or under construction."
- A *transfer station*. If the nearest dump is too far away to haul trash there economically, the garbage goes somewhere nearby to be compacted into large trailers for travelling the long distance
- A *processing plant*. These "materials recovery facilities" are transfer stations where recyclable materials get sorted out from the garbage, "densified" (e.g., crushed, shredded, baled), cleaned, and prepared for shipment.

WHAT'S A LANDFILL?

- In the mid-1930's, the first "sanitary landfills" were built in Fresno, California, and New York. These were really only open pit dumps, covered with dirt regularly to hide trash and cut down on flies, rats and odors.
- Most landfills are still just holes in the ground. Some are dug specifically for garbage, others are converted from old quarries and mines or from canyons.
- New landfills are lined on the bottom with either a big piece of plastic (like an extra-thick garbage bag), or dense soil.

HOW DOES IT WORK?

The structure of new landfills is like a beehive—the garbage is packed into cells.
- Each time a cell fills up, it's covered with dirt.
- Topsoil is added as a final covering so plants can grow to prevent erosion. Then the surface is graded so rainwater runs off.

$1 out of every $11 Americans spend for food goes for packaging.

WHAT'S GOING ON DOWN THERE?

• As it decomposes, garbage creates methane and sulfurous gases (which smell like rotten eggs). These gases are serious fire or explosion hazards. They also contribute to smog and/or global warming.

• In some newer landfills, pipes are sunk into the ground to control them. The gases are pumped out and either burned off or used to generate electricity.

• Landfill gas has even been used to carbonate soft drinks.

THE TOXIC SOUP

• A liquid called *leachate* is formed in landfills when water (from rain or underground springs) combines with decomposing garbage.

• Leachate is usually drained off into sewers or storm drains. It can seep into drinking water supplies.

• The exact danger posed by this potent brew isn't known. It contains many chemicals mixed together. The combined effect is unclear, but we *do* know we don't want it in our drinking water.

WHAT'S AN INCINERATOR?

• Incinerators are like gigantic state-of-the-art furnaces, run by computerized controls that rival the space shuttle (and cost about as much).

• They're sometimes called "waste to energy" plants, because when the trash burns, the heat can boil water into steam that turns a turbine to make electricity. The electricity they generate is often sold.

• They burn either: unprocessed trash, or a "fuel" made from trash by taking out the things that don't burn very well. This is not terribly efficient energy production. According to the Environmental Defense Fund, "Forty-five percent of mixed garbage doesn't burn, or burns poorly."

• Incinerators reduce the amount of trash that goes in by about 70%. The problem: The leftover 30% is highly toxic ash, which still has to be buried. The emissions are dangerous, too. According to one source, "Emissions from incinerator stacks have been known to include up to 27 heavy metals, acid gases, carbon monoxide, and dioxins."

The U.S. contributes 29% of the world's CFCs.

RECYCLING

BASICS

WHAT IS RECYCLING?

Y ou know the answer already, right? It's collecting your bottles, cans, and other materials and taking them to be recycled.
Unless you're a manufacturer, in which case recycling is what happens after materials have been collected.

...Or unless you're an art teacher who recycles old egg cartons and toilet paper rolls for school art projects.

You get the picture. Recycling is one of those words that everybody uses, and no one bothers to define. The result: It means different things to different people. That's okay, but how can we have a national dialogue about this significant issue if no one's speaking the same language?

So before we go any further, here's a handy reference guide to some uses of the word.

- **Official Definition:** The EPA calls recycling "collecting, reprocessing, marketing, and using materials once considered trash."

- **Classic Definition:** The same material is used over and over to make the same—or an equivalent—product. This cuts the amount of virgin materials required for manufacturing. Best examples: aluminum cans, glass bottles.

- **Plastics Definition:** One-way recycling. A plastic container is used once, then the material is used in a new, different item. This keeps the material out of landfills temporarily, but doesn't cut down on resources used to keep making the original product.

- **Manufacturer's Definition:** If a factory uses the same material twice, they feel they've recycled. The same goes if they use scraps (i.e. paper clippings leftover after envelopes are cut out).

- **Thrifty Definition:** Reusing something.

Don't forget: Aluminum foil is recyclable.

WHY RECYCLE?

I s recycling really worth the effort? Experts agree that it is—for many reasons.

THE GARBAGE GLUT

We've got to do something with all the garbage we produce.

• America produces an average of over a half a ton of garbage per person every year—about 3-1/2 pounds a day. And the figure is still growing.

• In a lifetime, the average American will throw away 600 times his or her adult weight in garbage. If you add it up, this means that a 150-lb. adult will leave a legacy of 90,000 lbs. of trash for his or her children.

NO MORE SPACE

Traditionally, we bury most of our garbage in landfills. But landfills are filling up and closing down all over the country.

• 70%, or 14,000, of America's 20,000 landfills closed between 1978 and 1988. By 1993, another 2,000 are expected to close.

SAFETY FIRST

Even if all landfills were available, they'd be health and safety hazards.

• Most landfills were built before safety standards became a high priority. They're not equipped to stop toxic leachate from seeping into the groundwater.

• How many landfills might eventually leak? According to the Environmental Protection Agency...*all* of them.

THE BURNING ISSUE

Burning garbage isn't the answer either.

• According to Environmental Action, "Even with pollution controls, incinerators are the largest new source of air pollution in most communities. They spew out gases that contribute to acid

---

13

rain, toxic heavy metals, and dioxins. And incinerators produce millions of tons of toxic ash, which still have to go to landfills."

IT'S COMMON SENSE
Making the most of what we've got is an American tradition.

Unlike landfills, which simply stockpile trash; or incineration, which leaves toxic ash to be disposed of, recycling removes waste completely, then turns it back into useful products.

IT'S QUICK
It takes less time than you think.

According to Recycle Now, "A study done for the EPA showed that the total time used by a householder is only 73 minutes—a little more than an hour—per month. That's a little over two minutes per day."

IT'S ECONOMICAL
Recycling is cheaper than landfilling or incineration. You can even make a profit on it.

• Some communities pay more to get rid of their trash than they do to maintain their police departments.

• Recycling saves towns and consumers money. When there's less garbage, we pay less to dump it.

• Individuals and businesses earn money by recycling. One family in Portland, Oregon, reportedly picked up enough aluminum cans along roads to pay for air fare to Hawaii. The Boeing Corporation has saved millions of dollars by recycling.

IT CAN SAVE NATURAL RESOURCES
Our resources are finite. If we don't recycle, we'll use them up.

• We can make aluminum from aluminum cans...or from an ore called bauxite. At the rate we're using up bauxite, the Earth will be completely stripped of it in 200-300 years.

• We can use old paper to make new paper...or just keep harvesting trees for virgin pulp. Every day, America cuts down two million trees—but throws away about 42 million newspapers.

Trash disposal costs the U.S. over $10 billion a year.

• We can re-refine old motor oil to make new motor oil...or keep using virgin oil to produce it. The known oil reserves in the world will only last an estimated 35 years at the rate we're using them.

IT SAVES ENERGY

One of the direct benefits of recycling is energy conservation
For example:

• Every year we save enough energy recycling steel to supply L.A. with nearly a decade's worth of electricity.

• Making one ton of recycled paper uses only about 60% of the energy needed to make a ton of virgin paper.

• We save enough energy by recycling one aluminum can to run a TV set for three hours.

• Recycling glass lowers the melting temperature for new glass, saving up to 32% of the energy needed for production.

There are indirect benefits to saving energy through recycling, as well.
For example:

• By using less energy, we protect pristine land from oil-drilling.

• Conserving energy reduces pollution from oil refineries.

• America imports about 50% of its oil. Saving energy by recycling means we depend less on foreign supplies.

IT HELPS SAVE THE RAIN FORESTS

We're all concerned about the rainforests. Recycling is a way to do something about it.

• According to *The Rainforest Book*, saving energy through recycling helps the rainforests by showing "the world that individual investments in energy efficiency can reduce the need to construct more dams and power plants for generating electricity. Dam construction in the rainforest accelerates deforestation."

• There's more: "Recycling your newspapers at home as well as white paper at the office will indirectly reduce the demand for both tropical and temperate timber."

A quarter of all aluminum goes into packaging.

RECYCLING & THE ENVIRONMENT

H ere are a few of the ways that recycling helps fight the environmental problems confronting us.

The Problem: The Greenhouse Effect

The world is getting hotter. One of the reasons: the "greenhouse effect," which is caused when gases like carbon dioxide (CO_2) and methane are released into the atmosphere. These gases act like the glass walls of a greenhouse; sunlight can get in, but heat can't get out.

Source: Carbon dioxide is released when coal, oil and natural gas, are burned by power plants, factories, and vehicles. Methane gas builds up when garbage decomposes in landfills, and is released upward through the trash.

The Connection: Recycling saves energy in the manufacturing process (e.g., a ton of recycled aluminum saves 95% of the energy needed to make new aluminum)—so less CO_2 is released.

• Recycling keeps trash out of landfills. Less trash, less gas.

• Trees "eat" CO_2. The more paper we recycle, the less trees we cut down. The end result? Less CO_2 means cleaner air.

The Problem: Water Pollution

More than half the people in the U.S. rely on groundwater as their drinking water. But groundwater is becoming polluted.

Source: Hazardous chemicals dumped by factories; used motor oil, antifreeze, and paint dumped by consumers; leachate in landfills that has mixed with rain; and more.

The Connection: Recycling hazardous waste keeps it out of our groundwater.

• Recycling means less leachate to pollute the water.

• Recycling means less industrial waste in the water. Recycling a

U.S. waste disposal is expected to cost 100 billion by the year 2000.

ton of office paper, for example, keeps 7,000 gallons of water out of the papermaking process. And it cuts down on bleaching, which means less dioxins in the water.

The Problem: Ozone Depletion

High above the earth there's a layer of ozone gas protecting us from the sun's harmful ultraviolet rays. This layer is being destroyed by manmade gases called chloroflourocarbons (CFCs and HCFCs). This is a threat to human health, crops, and wildlife.

Source: Air conditioners and refrigerators are among the main consumer uses of CFCs and HCFCs (they're coolants). They're also used as industrial solvents.

The Connection: If you recycle the coolant in your home or car air conditioner or refrigerator, you'll prevent the CFCs from escaping into the atmosphere.

• More solvents are needed to process raw materials than recycled ones. So the less products we make from virgin materials, the less solvents get used...and again, less CFCs.

The Problem: Soil Erosion

According to one estimate, the U.S. loses enough soil every year to fill 50 million boxcars. When this soil ends up in the water, it harms fish and pollutes our drinking water.

Source: Picture a forest after it's been clearcut. The trees that held the soil in place are gone, so it washes into lakes and streams.

The Connection: When we reuse paper and wood products, we have to cut down less trees...so more topsoil stays put.

The Problem: Acid Rain

Gases called sulfur oxides and nitrogen oxides are mixing with drops of moisture in the atmosphere. When the moisture falls as rain or snow, the acidic gases fall with it. In some places, the rain is now as acidic as lemon juice. It harms plants and wildlife.

Source: The gases are emitted by cars, factories and power plants when they burn fossil fuels (coal, oil, and natural gas).

The Connection: Recycling uses less energy in manufacturing processes, so it reduces the burning of fossil fuels...and acid rain.

Three million cars are abandoned every year in the U.S.

HOW IT'S DONE

S
o, are you going to take your recycling to a buyback or a drop-off? Have you thought about using a reverse-vending machine? Are you allowed to commingle? Do you have the slightest idea what we're talking about?

When recyclers refer to the different collection services that are available around the U.S., they often use terms most of us have never heard before. Don't let the words confuse you; they're really quite simple. Here's a quick guide to what they're all about.

CURBSIDE RECYCLING

• This is as easy as it gets—people come and pick up your recyclables at the curb, like your trash collector does. Pick-up can be once a week, every two weeks, or once a month.

• There are over 1,500 curbside programs in the U.S. They're so convenient that an estimated 65-80% of the people who are eligible take advantage of it. Wouldn't you?

• In most cases, curbside recycling isn't designed to make money—so there's a charge for the service. But even with the fees, it still usually costs considerably less than garbage disposal service...especially when you take into account that dumping or burning less garbage costs less.

A Few Curbside Details

• Most programs collect the basics: bottles, cans, and newspapers. A few also take plastic, cardboard, mixed paper, and motor oil.

• Some programs ask you to separate the materials into different categories. Others accept everything together, which is called "commingling" your recyclables.

• If you have curbside service, you'll receive bags, buckets, or bins to hold your recyclables. People in apartments usually get smaller bins, which are emptied into large cans or dumpsters in the garbage area of their complex.

• On collection day, materials are collected in special trucks or in bins attached to regular garbage trucks. Then they're unloaded at a central location and readied for shipping to processors.

The average baby generates a ton of garbage every year.

Note: Throughout this book we suggest contacting recycling centers to find out where to take your materials. If you're lucky enough to have curbside recycling, check with them first to find out what they accept.

RECYCLING DRIVES

• You're probably familiar with the short-term recycling projects that are generally run by non-profit groups like the Boy Scouts, Lion's Club, etc. They generally accept materials on a donation basis.

• By giving them your recyclables, you can do something for the community while helping them make money to support their cause.

HOUSEHOLD HAZARDOUS WASTE FACILITIES

• These special sites accept toxic materials—old paint, motor oil, antifreeze....They store the materials and dispose of them at a hazardous waste landfill, or send them to be recycled.

• Some communities don't have a permanent facility, but send around trucks on designated days to pick up hazardous materials.

DROP-OFF CENTERS

• "Drop-offs" are just that—places where you drop off your recyclables without being paid. They can be as simple as a few newspaper bins at an intersection, or as complex as a staffed recycling facility.

• At most drop-offs, you can usually leave your beverage containers, newspapers and corrugated cardboard. Some centers also accept other grades of paper, metals, used motor oil, and so on.

• Where do you find drop-offs? In convenient locations—grocery store parking lots, fire stations, vacant lots. You'll recognize them by the recycling logo and/or the logo of the sponsoring organization.

• These facilities are frequently open late. (In fact, some unstaffed centers, like the familiar bell-shaped recycling bins, are open 24-hours a day). They're simple—no weigh-ins, no lines, no hassle.

• Many landfills have drop-off centers near their entrances so people can recycle as much as possible before dumping trash.

• Drop-offs on wheels: In some communities, trucks drive to parking lots and wait for people to bring their recyclables to them.

• Who runs drop-offs? Charities, schools, churches, universities, town governments, and others. It's a long-term way to raise money.

The all-aluminum can was introduced in 1964.

BUYBACK CENTERS

• If you want to get paid for your recyclables, go to a buyback center. The pay rate varies—it's calculated to make a profit for the buyback operator, who sells the materials to brokers or manufacturers.

• Most buybacks are run by private companies with an eye on the bottom line. However, they're not all private enterprises. Cities subsidize some of them, and others are run by non-profit groups.

• Non-profit buybacks use donations to increase their revenues. Some will let you donate your share of the money to a charity of your choice.

• There are some 10,000 buybacks in the U.S. that specialize in aluminum cans—the most profitable item. Some of these buybacks have also branched out to accept other materials.

• Buybacks usually have limited hours, and you may have to wait in line while the operator weighs your cans and other materials.

• Where do you find a buyback? Try a supermarket parking lot. (In states with deposit laws, you redeem bottles and cans inside the store— but the buyback will take other materials outside).

• Buyback centers won't accept "contaminated" recyclables. For instance, cans or bottles filled with water or sand to make them weigh more are easily detected and rejected. Materials contaminated with grease, food, or hazardous substances, etc. are also turned away .

24-HOUR CAN-VENIENCE

• "Reverse vending machines" are automated buybacks that take back cans and pay you for them. What a concept! Most are found in states with deposit laws, and are sponsored by aluminum manufacturers.

COMPOSTING

• Composting is nature's way of recycling. If it's prepared right, organic material will break down into a rich "soil" that can be used as fertilizer or mulch. You can do it in your backyard. (See p. 71).

• Some communities have large-scale composting programs. Leaves and grass clippings are picked up at the curb. Other cities have compost centers at landfills, where you can drop off yard waste for less than what you'd pay at the landfill. Community gardens also usually compost, and often accept "donations."

GETTING

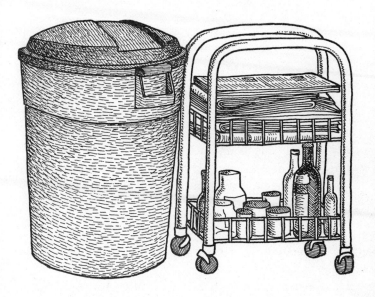

STARTED

HOW TO FIND A RECYCLING CENTER

I f there's no curbside recycling service where you live, you'll
have to go to a recycling center. In fact, even if you *do* have
curbside recycling, you may need one. Curbside service is usually limited to the basics—newspapers, cans, bottles—and most of
us have other things to recycle. Here are some ideas on where to
look for places to take what you've got.

CALL CITY HALL

• First, try your city or county government. So many people are
asking about recycling now that some government offices have
compiled lists of organizations and businesses which provide recycling. City governments almost always sponsor curbside recycling,
so they'll also be able to tell you if it's available where you live.

• Government departments to try (it varies by community): Public Works, Sanitation, Environmental Services. For household
hazardous waste sites (see p. 84), try Health or Environmental
Health.

• Another option: Your state recycling office may have a list of recycling centers. Find the address and phone number in the *Resources* section of this book (see p. 117).

• Even the most helpful governments may not know about *all*
the recyclers in your area—especially if you've got something other
than cans, bottles, and newspapers. So keep trying.

Here are some other sources:

THE PHONE BOOK

• Look in the Yellow Pages index under "Recycling" or "Recycling Centers."

• Also check these listings: "Salvage ," "Rubbish ," "Second-hand
Dealers," "Junk Dealers, " "Scrap Metals" and "Plastic, Used" (or
any "used" material.

Only 14% of all our trash was recycled in 1988.

ENVIRONMENTAL ORGANIZATIONS
• These groups may already have researched the recycling options in your area, and know the best ones. They may also be able to help you with"precycling." (see p. 29).
• Look in the Yellow Pages under "Environmental Groups."

STORES & SCHOOLS...
• Check around the community: Can you return things to the businesses that supplied them...or to others that will make use of them? For example: car batteries to service stations, coat hangers to dry cleaners, Styrofoam pellets to gift or pottery shops, and egg cartons or other materials to schools for art projects.

IF YOU OWN A BUSINESS
• The more bulk materials you have that can be recycled, the more sense it makes to find someone to collect them. Bonus: You may be able to save money by recycling.
• Where should you look? First contact your garbage company. See if they have a collection program for recyclables, and if they'll give you a price break (or pay you) for separating it. Example: Garbage collection companies routinely pick up corrugated cardboard.
• Check the phone book for recycling services. Note: Make sure you get references—these companies come and go all the time.

Special Cases
• If you have a small business (with less materials) and can't find a recycling service, see if your local government sponsors a recycling assistance program, or can refer you to other businesses that are recycling. Rhode Island, for example, helps small businesses combine their materials to attract a recycler. If nothing turns up locally, call your state recycling office.
• If you've got something unusual (like ink, photographic chemicals or cleaners) call your trade association—or one of its members—for recycling ideas.
• Help promote recycling: Send any information you turn up to your local government office. You'll be helping the next person who calls there looking for the same information.

Garbage Fact: If the Pilgrims had 6-packs, we'd still have the plastic rings from them today.

QUESTIONS TO ASK

When you find a recycling center, you'll need to know a few things about it. Here are some questions you can ask when you call, to be sure you make the most of the services available.

✔ *When are you open?*
A particularly good thing to know if you're taking recyclables to a drop-off. Some nonprofit drop-off locations are open 24 hours a day. Others schedule a recycling day once a week, or a few times a month.

✔ *What materials do you accept?*
All recycling centers are different. Some specialize—they'll only take the most profitable items, like aluminum cans. Others will take just about anything. If you can find a center that takes a variety of materials, ask for a printed list of what they accept. It can help avoid confusion.

✔ *How do you want the materials sorted or packaged?*
For example: Newspapers can be brought in loose, bagged, or tied—which do they prefer? Each recycling center has its own way of doing things, depending on what the companies they sell the materials to expect, how big their staff is, and what equipment they have. Ask for printed guidelines of their requirements.

✔ *How "clean" do the materials have to be?*
Should bottles and cans be rinsed out? Is it okay to include aluminum foil with cans? Should labels be removed from bottles? These are important questions—don't be afraid to ask them; it's the best way to avoid wasting time...and your recycled materials. Again, printed guidelines will make it easier.

✔ *How much do you pay for each material?*
If you want to be paid the highest price for your recyclables, compare prices at each place you call.

Note: A center that specializes in high-value materials like aluminum may be able to pay more for your recyclables because they're not subsidizing any lower value materials. But consider this: Recycling centers that take a variety of recyclables provide the greatest service to your community. Your high-value materials can help keep them in business.

Yard Waste makes up an estimated 18% of America's trash.

HOW TO SET UP AT HOME

O nce you've found out where your local recycling centers are and what they (or your curbside program) accept, you're ready to get down to business. Here are some ideas to help you get organized.

TAKE A LOOK IN THE TRASH

• What's in your garbage? Are things you normally throw away being recycled in your community? If you don't know, check it out at a local recycling center.

• Before you get into recycling, consider *pre*cycling (see p. 29). Change your buying habits to reduce garbage, or buy what *can* be recycled in your community. For example, plastic soda bottles can be recycled...but if there's no place to take them in your area, it's better to stick with aluminum or glass containers.

TAKE IT EASY

The most important part of setting up a home recycling program is to design it so it lasts. Don't try to recycle too many things in the beginning. Keep it manageable. If you've got a good system, then it will be easy to continue recycling.

GET YOUR FAMILY INVOLVED

Recycling works best if it's a family effort....so make an effort to get your family involved. Make them feel it's their program, too. For example, have your kids decorate cardboard boxes for storage bins; and ask them to suggest convenient spots to store the bins.

COME UP WITH A PLAN

• Decide how often you want to go to a recycling center.

• This will help you figure out how much storage space you need. If you recycle bottles once a week, for example, you'll need a lot less space than if you're taking them in once a month.

In 1865, an estimated 10,000 hogs roamed New York City, eating garbage.

• Be realistic about your schedule. Don't expect too much. Then try to stick to your plan. After a while recycling will become a habit—and you'll be doing it effortlessly.

STORAGE TIPS

• Figure out a convenient place (or places) to keep recyclables. It could be in your garage, under the sink, on the back porch, on a shelf in your basement, or in a closet or pantry.

• You may not need as much space as you think. *Recycle Now* points out: "Recycling actually takes only a small amount of space. Storage of cans, bottles, and newspapers for as long as a month takes around nine square feet of space."

• You don't have to store all your materials in one place. Whatever works is fine—but try to keep the storage spot for each material consistent, so people in your household always know where to put their recyclables.

LIMITED SPACE?

• A 2-step system may be the answer. You can keep small containers in your home or apartment, and empty them weekly into outside storage.

• In really tight spaces, you may have to limit your recycling to one or two materials. Don't let that bother you; just do what you can.

• Another suggestion: "Apartment owners and renters can get together to work out a community storage system for recyclables." (For more apartment ideas, see p. 108).

• Keep in mind: Choosing the right storage containers can make recycling in small areas easier. Also consider investing in some recycling supplies that will help you save space—for example, a can crusher.

BINS, BOXES...OR BAGS?

• If you're a curbside recycling customer, you've probably already got recycling bins. Otherwise, you need a storage system suited to your space and sense of aesthetics. That can be as simple as a couple of paper bags or as elaborate as a set of plastic stacking cartons.

Americans each use about 190 pounds of plastic per year.

• Containers with handles or straps make it easier to carry recyclables. Make sure they won't be too heavy to lift when they're full.

• Don't feel like lugging bins? Get a container on wheels.

• It sounds silly, but make sure the containers fit in your car.

• Containers should either be easily replaceable, like cardboard boxes, or washable.

• If you're recycling a number of materials (several kinds of paper, for example), think about investing in a set of stacking containers. Otherwise, you might have boxes all over the house.

NEAT TRICKS
One of the reasons people often give for not recycling is that it looks messy. What's the solution? Your recycling storage center may not be a work of art, but there are ways to make it tidy and convenient. Use your imagination; storing recyclables isn't a whole lot different than storing tools or other supplies.

A few container ideas:
• Sturdy cardboard liquor boxes
• Empty milk crates
• Plastic laundry baskets
• Prefer the natural look? Use rattan baskets.
• Plastic trash cans with lids (if you want to hide recyclables)
• Burlap or plastic weave "potato sacks"
• State-of-the-art recycling storage units (like cabinets with different compartments) are available in catalogs and storage supply shops. Or, just go to a department store and buy some easy-to-install shelves.

• Plastic stacking bins take up a minimum of floor space. Many are specially made for recycling. (See the list on the following page.) Alternative: inexpensive stackable storage cartons. Find them in office supply, hardware, and home furnishing stores.

• For paper: Keep a receptacle at your desk or where you open your mail. A small wicker wastebasket works fine.

• Limited floor space? Try hanging two or three canvas bags from hooks in a row.

During WW I, removing straps from corsets saved enough metal to build 2 warships.

RECYCLING SUPPLIES

Here are a few of the hundreds of companies that sell bins, bags, carts, and assorted recycling gadgets.

The Bag Connection, P.O. Box 817, Newberg, OR 97132; (800) 62-BAGIT, (503) 538-3211. *The "BAGIT" is a woven plastic bag available in three strengths; $1.17 to $2.75 per bag.*

Bundle Buddy c/o Continental Business Initiatives, 4435 Nobel Dr., Suite 6, San Diego, CA 92122; (619) 450-1231. *This device makes tying newspapers easy, and it can also bundle magazines. About $15.*

Co-op America, 2100 M St., Suite 403, Washington, D.C. 20063; (800) 424-2667. *14-gallon bins, recycling carts that fit 2 or 3 bins.*

Eco-Choice, P.O. Box 281, Montvale, NJ 07645; (800) 535-6304. *A hinged recycling chest made to fit two grocery bags; $16.00. Corrugated cardboard bins with tops; $5.75 each.*

Gordon's Blueprints for Recycling, 163 Engle St., Englewood, NJ 07631. *Complete plans for building a home recycling storage system; $17.50.*

Real Goods, 966 Mazzoni Rd., Ukiah, CA 95482; (800) 762-7325. *Stackable, heavy-duty plastic bins in red, white, green; 3 for $36.*

Roberta Fortune's Almanac, 150 Chestnut St., San Francisco, CA 94111. *A variety of home recycling supplies.*

Sensible Supplies, 332 Highland Ave., Winchester, MA 01890; (617) 729-3917. *Plastic stacking crates, cardboard containers and reusable bags.*

7th Generation, Dept. P04300, Colchester, VT 05446-1672; (800) 441-2538. *Stackable plastic bins made from recycled tires and plastic; $13.95 each.*

Reusable glass containers make about 15 trips between factories and stores before being recycled.

A WORD ABOUT PRECYCLING

I n 1989, the city government of Berkeley, California initiated a campaign to encourage consumers to buy food packaged in recyclable materials. They called it *Precycling*.

"We *recycle* items after we've bought them," they explained. We can *precycle* while we shop. What we buy has a direct relationship to what we throw away…So it's time we took a serious look at what we take home in the first place. Why not reduce waste by *not* buying something? …This may just be the easiest way to help save the Earth. Simply by making correct buying choices, by *precycling*, we can prevent excessive and unsound materials from getting into our waste stream. The consumer buck stops here. With us."

It was a good idea in 1989—and it's an even better idea today…not only in supermarkets, but wherever we shop. Packaging makes up about a third of what Americans throw away; and it's a luxury we can't afford. As far as EarthWorks is concerned, precycling is an integral part of any recycling effort.

PRECYCLING TIPS

The key to precycling: think ahead. Figure out how you're going to dispose of a product—and its packaging—before you buy it.

• Think of packaging as part of the product. You get what you pay for: If the packaging is designed to be thrown away immediately, all you're getting for your money is cleverly-designed garbage.

• The National Recycling Coalition suggests: "In the store, you may ask, 'Is it nutritious? Is it fattening?' Now ask: 'How is it packaged?'"

• Look for containers that can be reused or recycled, like aluminum and glass, or ones that can be composted, like paper.

• Buy in bulk whenever you can—everything from beans to hardware is available without packaging.

• Avoid items that are made to be thrown away after only a few uses, like some razors and flashlights. Look for products you can use over and

Many companies own their own forests.

over again—thermos jars, rechargeable batteries, sponges, and so on.

• Avoid buying products that contain hazardous materials, which are difficult to dispose of safely.

• Use cloth shopping bags instead of paper or plastic.

USE YOUR INFLUENCE

You may not think that one opinion can help change the way products are packaged, but don't sell yourself short. You have influence.

• The Pennsylvania Resources Council says: "When we spend our money, we 'vote' for the products that reflect our values. In environmental shopping, every individual's participation does make a difference."

• John Ruston, of EDF, says: "Keep pushing citizen activism....Proctor & Gamble, Colgate, etc. spend millions just to gain 1% market share increases—they will listen!"

• And we all know what happens when products stay on the shelf too long: They're replaced with better ones.

SPEAK UP

If you're not happy about the packaging you see at the supermarket:

• The National Recycling Coalition suggests: "If you can't find recyclable packaging, let the manager know you want it. Ask if the store sells its own brands in recyclable packaging."

• Ask them to start their own recycling campaign.

• Write to your state and federal officials to support legislation favoring recycling and packaging reduction.

• Fill out customer comment cards and request that stores only accept products with minimal and ecologically sound packaging.

• Many products have toll-free telephone numbers printed on the outside in case people have any questions. If you think something is poorly packaged (i.e. like one breakfast's-worth of pancake mix in a plastic squeeze bottle), call the company and say so.

• Buy recycled products (see page 113).

SOURCES

The Green Consumer Letter, Tilden Press, Inc., 1526 Connecticut Ave. N.W., Washington, D.C. 20036; (800) 955-GREEN. *A monthly newsletter with the latest info on earth-postive consumer products, $27.00.*

Newspaper pulp starts out as 99% water and 1% fiber.

METAL

DON'T CAN IT

In America, 1,500 aluminum cans are recycled every second.

For the recycling novice—in other words, almost all of us—aluminum cans are as close to perfect as you can get: No matter how many of them you have, they're still light enough to carry; you don't need any fancy storage containers—you can even pile them into a paper bag. And you don't have to hunt very far to find someplace to take them—cans are worth so much that there's always someone around who collects them.

The secret is that it's a lot cheaper to recycle aluminum cans than it is to make them out of new metal. So years ago, the aluminum industry set up collection services, and they've been paying top dollar to get cans back ever since.

So if you're wondering where to start recycling, put aluminum cans at the top of your list.

ALUMINATING FACTS

• Aluminum was worth more than gold when it was discovered. It was first used to make a rattle for Napoleon's son.

• In 1989, Americans used 80 billion aluminum cans. That's the equivalent of about 16 cans for every person on the planet.

• We recycled a record 60% of them that same year.

• Making cans from recycled aluminum cuts related air pollution (for example, sulfur dioxides, which create acid rain) by 95%.

• Recycling aluminum saves 95% of the energy used to make the material from scratch. That means you can make *20* cans out of recycled material with the same energy it takes to make *one* can out of new material.

• Americans throw away enough aluminum every three months to rebuild our entire commercial air fleet.

SIMPLE THINGS TO DO

1. Find a Place to Take Them

• Virtually all recycling programs accept aluminum cans. But not

Which state recycles the most? Washington.

everyone takes other types of aluminum (foil and scrap). Call recycling centers in your area for more details.

• If you're having trouble finding a recycling center, try the toll-free Reynolds Aluminum hotline: (800) 228-2525. If there's a Reynolds recycling center in your area, they'll tell you where it is.

• Check phone listings under "Scrap Metal." Many scrap dealers aren't interested in small loads, but aluminum is valuable—so they may take it.

• Contact your state recycling office (listed in the back of this book). They may have a list of aluminum recyclers in the state.

3. Recycle

Cans

• Crushing cans makes storing and transporting them easier. But before recycling, check with your recycler to find out if crushing them is okay. In some states with deposit laws, recyclers prefer to get the cans intact; they need to see the brand and the name of the factory the can came from.

• In most places, it's not necessary to rinse cans...but a large batch of unwashed cans may attract bees and ants.

Foiled Again

• Aluminum foil, pie plates, TV dinner trays, etc. are all reusable and recyclable. Lightly rinse them off first if they're dirty (you don't have to waste water—use dishwater).

• Some places request that you keep foil and cans separate. Check with your local recycling center.

Other Items

• Containers aren't the only source of aluminum scrap. Other common items include window frames, screen doors and lawn furniture. However, check with your recycling center before including these.

• Is your scrap aluminum? Check it with a magnet; aluminum isn't magnetic. Check small pieces like screws, rivets, etc.

• Remove everything that's not aluminum.

FOR MORE INFORMATION

"Aluminum Recycling: America's Environmental Success Story." The Aluminum Association, 900 19th St., N.W., Washington, D.C. 20006. (202) 862-5100.

TIN SIMPLE THINGS YOU CAN DO

Every day Americans use enough steel and tin cans to make a steel pipe running from Los Angeles to New York...and back again.

After aluminum cans, what's next?

How about tin cans.?...You know—the ones pet foods, tomato paste, soup, pork & beans and other foods come in.

Tin cans are just as easy to melt down and reuse as aluminum, and recycling them can save an incredible amount of resources: If we only recycled *one-tenth* of the cans we now throw away, we'd save about 3.2 billion of them every year. That's a lot of steel, mining waste and landfill space.

Why haven't you heard more about this? Money. Manufacturers haven't been paying very much for cans. But that's starting to change. And when the price gets high enough, tin cans will become a recycling staple.

PLAY IT AGAIN, SPAM

• Tin cans are actually 99% steel, with a thin layer of tin added to prevent rusting.

• Recycling steel and tin cans saves 74% of the energy used to produce them from raw materials.

• At least 70-80% of the tin on a can is saved when you recycle it. This cuts down mining waste and preserves a valuable resource.

• Americans use 100 million tin and steel cans every day.

SIMPLE THINGS YOU CAN DO

1. Find a Place to Take Them

• Call your local recycling center. Recyclers don't make enough money on tin cans to pay consumers yet, but often accept and recycle the cans anyway.

• Outside chance: A scrap metal dealer might take them. If you want to try, look in the Yellow Pages under "Scrap metal."

• If you can't find a place, contact the Steel Can Recycling Institute or your state recycling office (listed in back of this book).

2. Store Them

• Store steel cans the way you store aluminum. But unless your local recycling program instructs you to "commingle," keep the two materials separate.

• It's often hard to tell if a can is aluminum or steel. Some cans even have steel bodies and aluminum lids. They're called "bi-metal;" you can include them with steel cans.

• The easiest way to tell if it's steel: Use a refrigerator magnet to test it. Check the body *and* the lids. (Steel is magnetic, aluminum isn't.) Note: If it has ribs on the side, it's steel.

3. Recycle

• If you haven't already, take off the lids with a can opener. This makes the can bodies crushable. (Flat cans save space.)

• Turn the can on its side and step on it. (It's easier than it sounds—it doesn't have to be perfectly flat.) If the lids are steel, you can put them inside the flattened can body.

• It's hard to flatten pet food and tuna cans because they have a round lip on the bottom. They can be recycled intact.

• Should you remove the labels? The rules vary from state to state. Call your recycling center to find out.

What About Aerosol Cans?

• Although empty aerosol cans are technically recyclable, recyclers say they're extremely difficult and expensive for recyclers to dispose of. Their propellants are usually flammable and have been known to explode in garbage trucks. Solution: Avoid buying them.

FOR MORE INFORMATION

"The Recycling Magnet." A newsletter from the Steel Can Recycling Institute, Foster Plaza 10, 680 Andersen Dr., Pittsburgh, PA 15220. Call (800) 876-SCRI. *They also have brochures.*

One person uses two pine trees' worth of paper products each year.

STEEL AWAY

In 1988, about 9 million steel automobile bodies—more than the U.S. auto industry produced that year—were recycled.

You're probably not ecstatic about lugging an old swing set to a recycling center or scrap metal dealer. We don't blame you... But consider the alternatives: You can haul it to the dump, where it'll become part of the garbage crisis...or you can leave it around and watch it rust.

Okay, maybe you don't have a swing set. How about an old bike frame or a rusty bucket? They can be recycled, too.

The only problem is—and it's the same one we keep running into—there aren't enough people who'll take what you've got. Scrap dealers, the traditional steel recyclers, are usually more interested in industrial scrap (which brings in more money) than single items from individuals.

But don't give up. Some scrap dealers will happily accept your steel cast-offs. So will some recycling centers. Look for them—they're out there.

WHY RECYCLE?

• Americans throw out enough iron and steel to supply all the nation's automakers on a continuous basis.

• According to the American Iron and Steel Institute, steel recycling saves the U.S. over $2 billion a year in landfill disposal costs alone—about $8 for every man, woman and child in America.

• A steel mill using recycled scrap reduces related water pollution, air pollution and mining wastes by about 70%.

• It takes about four times as much energy to make steel from virgin ore as it does to make the same steel from scrap. Annually, enough energy is saved by recycling steel to supply the city of Los Angeles with almost a decade's worth of electricity.

SIMPLE THINGS TO DO
1. Find a Place to Take It

• Most scrap dealers will take steel, but not all will take small

During the last decade, world steel makers recycled almost 2.5 billion tons of steel.

"household" amounts—some buy only huge quantities. Look in the Yellow Pages under "Recycling" or "Scrap Metal." Call around.

2. Stash Your Steel

• Most steel items are one-shot recyclables; you won't have a steady supply. Store them in an out-of-the-way recycling spot (the garage or basement is fine) until you're ready to recycle.

3. Recycle

• Household items, including: folding chairs, fencing, broken tools, play equipment, plumbing fixtures, bike frames, garbage cans, ducts and vents, etc. Iron items can be recycled with steel.

• Remove everything except steel (wood, cloth, plastic, aluminum, etc.) If you're not sure it's steel, use a magnet to check; steel is magnetic. Don't worry about rust. It won't affect recycling.

Other Items

• Paint cans are now accepted by many steel recyclers, but paint is a "hazardous waste"—so if the cans contain too much paint residue, local recyclers may not accept them. Call first to find out.

• Clothes hangers: Local recycling centers may not take them because they're a low grade of steel; call first. Alternative: Give them to dry cleaners or 2nd-hand stores; each should gladly accept them.

• Water heaters are good scrap, but recyclers may want the insulation material that sits between the tank and sheet metal skin removed. Call to find out. For other appliances, see p. 94.

Cars

• What most Americans think of as "junkyards" are actually efficient car recycling centers. After recovering saleable parts, junk dealers separate leftover components by type of material—steel, aluminum, copper, zinc, glass and various plastics—for recycling.

• The remaining "hulk" is flattened and sent to scrap dealers. Metal recovered this way accounts for about 1/3 of U.S. steel scrap.

FOR MORE INFORMATION
"Recycling Scrap Iron and Steel." Institute of Scrap Recycling Industries, Inc., 1627 K Street, N.W., Washington, D.C. 20006-1704. (202) 466-4050.

The average person generates 8 pounds of newspaper in a month.

LOST & FOUNDRY

Enough scrap copper was recycled in the U.S. in 1989 to supply the wiring and plumbing for every building constructed here that year.

Want to test your metal mettle? There's always more to recycle. How about stainless steel sinks? Hinges? Old plumbing? Pipes? Here are a few other ideas.

SIMPLE THINGS YOU CAN DO

1. Find a Recycler
• If the metal's only good for scrap, check "Scrap Metals" in the Yellow Pages. Or give it to a plumber or electrician who recycles.
• If it's reuseable, call a salvage yard.

2. Recycle

Stainless Steel
• Stainless steel contains at least 10% chromium, so it can't be recycled with standard steel.
• Cookware is often stainless. It's also highly valued by second-hand stores, so the best way to recycle it is to donate it.
• There's more stainless steel in your home than you think; we tend to hold onto things that look good, even after they're hopelessly broken. Some items you'll find around the house: silverware, sinks, some window frames, appliances and hand tools.

Copper
• Copper is a prized scrap metal found in plumbing, telephone and utility wiring, and car radiators. Most is recovered from businesses, not individuals.

Brass
• Also a prized scrap metal. Keep it separate from copper. You'll find it in: plumbing fixtures and pipes, fireplace tools, screws, door-knobs, and hinges.

FOR MORE INFORMATION
"Recycling Nonferrous Scrap Metals." Institute of Scrap Recycling Industries, Inc., 1627 K Street, N.W., Washington, D.C. 20006-1704. (202)466-4050.

Which state has the most landfills? Texas.

GLASS

GLASSIFIED INFORMATION

*Americans throw away enough glass bottles and jars every two weeks
to fill the 1,350-foot towers of the World Trade Center.*

I t's interesting to listen to people talk about why they like glass.
The appeal is more than just being able to recycle it easily—
they like the way it looks and feels, too.

It's an ancient attraction. Glass bottles and jars have been a part
of human culture for more than 3,000 years. We've been recycling
them just about that long, too. In fact, it's conceivable that some of
the glass you'll use today was once part of a bottle used by Richard
the Lion-Hearted or Catherine the Great.

Of course it's not likely, but so what? The point is that recycling
glass is a time-honored tradition. It's up to us to keep it going for
the next 3,000 years.

A TOUCH OF GLASS

• Before recycled glass is shipped to manufacturers, it's broken so
it'll take up less space. This broken glass is called "cullet."

• When it arrives at the glass factory, the cullet is run through a
device which removes metal rings from bottles. A vacuum process
removes plastic coatings and paper labels.

• When it's "clean," the cullet is added to raw materials and melted down with them. Most bottles and jars contain at least 25% recycled glass.

• Glass never wears out—it can be recycled forever.

WHY RECYCLE?

• We save over a ton of resources for every ton of glass recycled. (If
you want specifics, it's 1,330 pounds of sand, 433 pounds of soda
ash, 433 pounds of limestone, and 151 pounds of feldspar.)

• A ton of glass produced from raw materials creates 384 pounds of

Recycling data: A 12-inch stack of newspaper weighs 35 lbs.

mining waste. Using 50% recycled glass cuts it by about 75%.

• We get 27.8 pounds of air pollution for every ton of new glass produced. Recycling glass reduces that pollution by 14-20%.

• Recycling glass saves 25-32% of the energy used to make glass.

• Glass makes up about 8% of America's municipal garbage.

SIMPLE THINGS YOU CAN DO

1. Precycle

• Look for refillable bottles. They're the most energy and material efficient; they can be sterilized and reused up to seven times before recycling.

• Refillables aren't easy to find any more. But if enough consumers speak up at local supermarkets, they'll reappear on shelves. Case in point: Washington's Rainier Brewery, citing its customers' environmental concerns, has recently returned to using refillables for all its single serving bottles.

• An easy way to manage refillables: Get one of the sturdy crates they come in, and store "empties" in it. When the crates are full, take them to the store and exchange the empties for full bottles.

• In some areas of the Midwest and Mountain states, glass is not accepted because there's no market for it. In these areas, consider buying aluminum cans, which are recycled virtually everywhere.

2. Store It

• It's safer to pack bottles in boxes or bins than in bags.

• Don't leave the bottles in six-pack carriers; that makes extra processing work for recyclers (they have to remove the bottles).

• If you're selling your glass at a buyback center or dropping it off, you'll probably have to separate it into brown, green and clear glass. The reason: To make recycling profitable, glass factories need to turn brown glass into brown bottles, etc. If colors are mixed, the end product is an unpredictable hue. Glass factories don't like it because their orders are for specific colors.

• If you have any blue or other colored glass containers, recycle them with the brown or green glass—but only in small amounts.

Which state burns the most garbage? Connecticut (67%).

- If the glass is even slightly tinted, sort as colored, not as clear.
- Broken bottles can be recycled, but not everyone accepts them.
- Curbside programs generally accept all colors mixed together; sorting occurs later. Keep glass unbroken if possible—it's easier for the recycling crew to handle.

3. Recycle

- Remove lids and caps. You can recycle steel caps with steel cans. (Plastic cap liners are no problem). For aluminum caps, check with the recycling center before including them with aluminum cans.
- It's okay to leave on neck rings, paper and plastic labels—they burn or blow off in the recycling process.
- Dump out food residue and lightly rinse bottles. Old food attracts animals, it's a mess for recyclers, and it stinks. Be sure to empty beer bottles. A drop of beer can turn into a slimy mold.
- Remove rocks and dirt from bottles found in parks, beaches, etc. Even a little stone can ruin a whole load of glass.

4. Absolutely Don't Include...

- Windows, drinking glasses, mirrors, Pyrex (baking dishes, coffee pots, etc.), or other glass. Any of these can ruin an entire batch of glass if they slip through at the factory. The reason: They don't melt at the same temperature as bottles.
- Ceramics (coffee mugs, mustard jars, plates, etc.). They don't melt down with the glass, so they contaminate it.

IF YOUR STATE HAS A "BOTTLE BILL..."

- Not all states accept the same bottles for redemption. Some take only beer and soft drink bottles; others include juice or liquor bottles. Check with stores or recycling centers.
- General Rules: Empty bottles; you may need to sort them by brand to get your deposit back. Broken bottles aren't redeemable.

SOURCES
"Glass Recycling: Why? How?" The Glass Packaging Institute, 1801 K St. N.W., Suite 1105-L, Washington, D.C. 20006.

If tin cans were really made of tin, you could crush them with your hand.

TAKING PANES

*More than a million tons of plate glass, mirrors, test
tubes and light bulbs are thrown away every year.*

When you break a window, can you recycle it? Not necessarily. It may come as a surprise, but the glass in windows and most "other" glass is different than the pure glass in bottles and jars. For example, plate glass contains a chemical called *boron*; car windshields contain plastic; crystal contains lead; mirrors are backed with silver. This makes recycling complicated, but people are working on it. Before long, it won't be such a pane in the glass.

A TOUCH OF GLASS

• About 4% of the waste in landfills is "other" glass.

• Most "other" glass recycling is done by manufacturers who remelt production scraps. It's easy for them because they have large quantities of the same type of glass.

• Light bulbs can't be recycled. Neither can mirrors, or crystal.

• The most important new recycling opportunity for "other" glass is as an *aggregate*. Aggregates are bulk materials such as gravel or sand, which are used as fill or underbedding in road construction. New York City is currently using 12 truckloads of "other" glass every day in its Asphalt Green recycling plant in Manhattan.

SIMPLE THINGS YOU CAN DO

1. Reuse

• If a window is still intact, see if you can bring it to a salvage yard.

2. Recycle

• Some recycling processors handle plate glass as a specialty item. Check the Yellow Pages under "Recyclers." Call ahead to find out.

• In some parts of the country window glass is being collected and used in fiberglass. If they're doing this in your area, make sure wood and metal are removed before recycling.

Every day, Americans spend $250,000 getting rid of old tires.

PAPER

THE PAPER CHASE

"To tree or not to tree?" That is the question.

HOW IS PAPER MADE?
A pulp "soup" is concocted by boiling wood chips, water and chemicals together in an industrial-size blender. This separates wood fibers from *lignin*—the "glue" that holds the wood together. Then, the fibers are beat into something that looks like oatmeal.
• Next, the mix is bleached—often repeatedly—with chlorine (unless it's brown paper like cardboard). Chlorine bleaching produces dioxins. According to one source, "Modern pulp and paper production technology creates some of the most toxic effluent any industry can produce." But that's beginning to change: A few companies are starting to use non-chlorine bleach as an alternative.
• Starch is added to make the fibers bond together, the paper is dried on a moving screen, and then wound onto a giant spool.

HOW IS IT RECYCLED?
Back in the blender, shredded bales of paper are mixed with warm water, heated and mashed into pulp.
• Paper clips and string are strained out and any ink is dissolved with a solvent and removed. Then it's bleached again, but less bleach is required, since the pulp has already been whitened once. Sometimes alternatives to chlorine bleach are used.
• Paper can be recycled up to 7 times, depending on how long fibers are to begin with.

IS ALL PAPER RECYCLED THE SAME WAY?
• There are special considerations for each type of paper, but basically, it's the same process for all of them.
• For example, glossy paper requires special handling, while environmentally friendly "minimum impact" recycled paper skips the ink-dissolving and bleaching stages.

HOW MUCH PAPER ARE WE TALKING ABOUT?
Literally reams and reams: At least 40% (some experts estimate as high as 50%) of the U.S. waste stream is paper; that's about 88 million tons per year. We recycle between 25-30% of our paper.

Activist Tim McClure staked a mining claim on a landfill to dramatize the need for recycling.

OLD NEWS IS GOOD NEWS

*Americans throw away the equivalent of more
than 30 million trees in newsprint each year.*

I f you're one of the millions of Americans who are recycling your
newspapers, here's some good news: You're making a big difference.

Not only are you saving natural resources and landfill space,
you're helping to change the way the paper industry works.

Until recently, newspaper publishers believed that recycling was
just a fad—that we'd "get over it." Now it's clear that Americans
are committed...So they're going to give us what we want.

RECYCLING NEWS

• Every day Americans buy about 62 million newspapers...and
throw out around 44 million of them. That means the equivalent
of about 500,000 trees is dumped into landfills every week.

• If we recycled just half our newsprint every year, we'd need
3,200 fewer garbage trucks to collect our trash.

• If you recycled the *New York Times* every day for a year, you'd
prevent 15 pounds of air pollution. That doesn't sound like much,
but it adds up. If everyone who subscribes to the *New York Times*
recycled, we'd keep over 6,000 *tons* of pollution out of the air.

• According to *Clean Ocean Action*, recycling a 36"tall stack of
newspaper saves the equivalent of about 14% of the average household electric bill.

• Top uses for recycled newsprint: More newsprint, paperboard.
Also, construction paper, insulation, egg cartons, animal bedding.

PILES OF PAPER

• One of the results of America's new enthusiasm for recycling is a
"newspaper glut." More paper on the market means lower prices.
This is bad for collection programs, but good for mills.

• Of the 25 newsprint mills in the U.S., only ten of them can recycle. Most of our newsprint is manufactured in Canada, and only two of the 42 newsprint mills there are set up to recycle. However, many have announced plans to recycle; some are beginning.

• It may be a while before mills catch up to the public. It takes about 18 months and $40-80 million to retool a mill to recycle.

• Does this mean we shouldn't bother recycling? No, no, no. Mill-owners and newspapers have been waiting to see if recycling is a legitimate trend before they make major investments. But because we've kept the pressure up, they're making the necessary adjustments.

SIMPLE THINGS YOU CAN DO

1. Find a Recycling Center
• It should be easy. Most recyclers accept newspaper, including curbside programs, recycling centers, charity paper drives, etc.

2. Recycle
• Ask your recycling center or curbside service if newspapers should be tied or left loose.

• If they should be tied, put them in bundles about 10" thick, so they're easy to carry. Tying tip: Lay the string in an empty box with the ends draping out over the sides. Put the paper in the box and make the knot.

• If they should be left loose, store the papers in brown grocery bags or cardboard boxes.

• Don't worry about pulling out all the glossy inserts, but don't *add* any junk mail or magazines to the pile. Try to keep the paper dry.

• If you're taking the newspaper to a recycling center, you may be asked to empty out the bags or cut the strings holding the bundles; some recyclers prefer just the newspaper.

• Don't recycle newspaper you've used for birdcages, for house-breaking your dog, or for painting or art projects.

FOR MORE INFORMATION
"Read, Then Recycle." American Newspaper Publishers Association, The Newspaper Center, 11600 Sunrise Valley Drive, Reston, VA 22091; (703) 648-1125. A *free pamphlet*.

Dog food bags can't be recycled; they have plastic linings inside.

CORPORATE STOCK

Americans discard 4 million tons of office paper every year—enough to build a 12-foot-high wall of paper from New York to California.

Since it's all we usually hear about, you might assume that newspaper is the most valuable paper to recycle. But it's not. The most valuable—by far—is office paper.

Oh, great. Now we want you to recycle at work, too?

Well, suppose we told you it would make your business money... and save garbage fees...and save up to 1-1/2 trees per person every year?

And that's just the beginning.

BUSINESS NEWS

• Americans throw out about 85% of the office paper we use.

• Office paper is prized by recyclers because it's made with strong fibers that hold up well the second time around.

• White paper is worth twice as much (or more) as colored ledger paper.

• Office paper has already been bleached, and there's not much ink on it that has to be removed (compared to newspapers). As a result, recyclers only have to use 25% as much bleach as the manufacturers used. This cuts down on dioxins in our water. In addition, some recycled bleaching processes don't use chlorine-based chemicals.

• Recycling printing and writing paper saves 33% of the energy needed to make it from trees. It conserves resources too. For example, every time we recycle a ton of it, we save 7,000 gallons of water.

SIMPLE THINGS YOU CAN DO

1. Precycle

• Consider using white paper for all office forms—even legal pads, which don't have to be yellow, and message slips, which don't have to be pink. That will reduce sorting, and make the scrap more valuable.

Glass makes up 8% of trash thrown out by U.S. households.

2. Where To Take It?

• Most recycling centers will accept office paper. It's the highest grade of paper, and the easiest to recycle.

• Ask your garbage haulers if they have an office collection program.

• Look in the Yellow Pages under "Waste Paper" or "Recycling" to find a company that picks up loads of office stock (See p. 48.)

3. Recycle

White Paper

• This includes: white computer paper, typing paper, stationery (letterhead and bond), index cards, copier paper. Note: Not all mills accept paper that's been printed with a laser printer. Ask your local recycler.

• Envelopes are fine if they have water soluble glue. "Lick-to-stick" glue is okay. But no plastic windows (rip the plastic out) or adhesive labels (the glue is a contaminant).

• Writing with colored ink is no problem; it doesn't affect recycling.

• Staples, paper clips are okay; but remove larger clips and fasteners.

• Non-paper items like plastic, cigarette butts, styrofoam coffee cups, etc. should be kept out of the white paper bin.

Colored Office Paper

• Sometimes it can't be added to the white paper—the fiber has been dyed, and the dye is a contaminant. Check with your local recycler.

• No construction paper. Add it to your "mixed paper" (see p. 55).

Computer Paper

• This is that oversized computer paper with green bars printed on it. If you only have a little, put it in with the white paper. If you've got a lot, keep it separate. It's the highest grade of paper; you'll get top dollar.

Don't Recycle

• Anything with adhesives. This usually includes "post-it" notes and mailing address labels (i.e., "pressure sensitive" ones—again, "lick to stick" glue is okay). Tear off labels before recycling.

• Fax paper, NCR paper (carbonless copies), or blueprints; they have chemical coatings.

SOURCES
"Office Paper Recycling Kit." Conservatree Paper Company, 10 Lombard St., Suite 250, San Francisco, CA 94111 (415) 433-1000. *An introductory packet of articles and fact sheets; $12.*

Between 1960 & 1984, the number of soda containers in America's garbage tripled.

RE-BOX:
JUST DO IT

Every year, we use the equivalent of 120 corrugated cardboard boxes for every American.

Y ou probably don't care much about cardboard boxes unless you're moving, or if you have to store a bunch of old books. But recyclers love to get their hands on them.

Believe it or not, corrugated cardboard boxes are really valuable. The paper fibers are long and strong, and they can be recycled many times.

Of course, you probably don't get enough boxes to become a big-time cardboard recycler, but if each American household recycled even one per month, we'd save more than a billion boxes a year. That's a lot of trees...with just a little effort.

THE BOXING MATCH

• When people in the recycling business talk about cardboard, they mean *corrugated* cardboard, which is made from brown kraft paper (The other kind—cereal boxes, etc.—is called boxboard).

• Corrugated cardboard is made by sandwiching a layer of fluted paper between two flat sheets of paper, and then gluing all three together.

• Americans use enough cardboard each year to make a bale as big as a football field, and as high as the World Trade Center.

• We recycle about half the corrugated we use—more than any other paper product. The secret of our success: Stores and businesses use and recycle a steady stream of boxes.

• Most corrugated boxes contain 20 percent recycled material. Manufacturers predict that figure will soon be up to 40 percent.

• Making the paper pulp used in cardboard creates sulfur dioxide, a gas that causes acid rain. Recycling cuts that pollution in half.

• By recycling cardboard, we save about 1/4 of the energy used to manufacture it.

The U.S. has over 1,000 municipal composting programs.

SIMPLE THINGS TO DO

1. Find a Recycler

• Local recycling centers generally accept corrugated. Curbside recyclers may take it, too—but they'll probably want it tied up.

• In urban areas, paper brokers will pay for large amounts of corrugated. Look them up in the Yellow Pages.

• If there's no alternative, check with a local grocery chain—they have balers and reclaim all their cardboard; they may let you add your boxes to theirs.

2. Store It

• Recyclers *will* take one box at a time, but it's not really convenient. You'll probably want to store boxes until you've got a bunch, then drop them all off together.

• Put a big box aside, then flatten the others and stuff them inside it. To flatten: Pull the box apart where it's taped or glued together, and let it fold flat naturally.

• Flattened boxes can be bound together with twine, but the twine will have to be removed at the recycling center.

3. Recycle

• First, remove any contents and foreign materials—like foam packing, plastic, string, wire, wood (some boxes are partly made of wood). Pull tape off, too.

• If you're recycling corrugated pizza boxes: Clean off the food first. If they're really greasy, it's better to throw them away.

• Don't mix waxed corrugated boxes with the regular corrugated. They aren't recyclable. Once paper fibers are impregnated with wax, they can't be reclaimed.

• You can recycle wet boxes.

Note: Brown paper bags can be recycled with cardboard.

FOR MORE INFORMATION

"Reducing Corrugated Cardboard Waste." Office Waste Reduction Services, Michigan Department of Commerce, P.O. Box 30004, Lansing, MI 48909 (517) 335-1178. *A free fact sheet.*

About 75% of America's glass is used for packaging.

PROFIT & GLOSS

In 1989, magazine publishers used enough paper to supply 5 billion doctors' offices with a one-year subscription to Garbage *magazine.*

W hat magazines do you subscribe to? *Time? Newsweek? Vogue? Sports Illustrated?* Take a look at the paper they're printed on; it's glossy, and smooth, and looks like it costs a lot...Right? That's why they use it.

Here's the frustrating part—it turns out that glossy paper is hard to recycle. Why? It's coated with clay, which turns into sludge in the recycling process.

Sorry to give you bad news; we can't gloss it over.

But there's good news, too. Americans read so many magazines every year that recyclers are starting to find a way to use them.

SHINE IT ON

• One reason recyclers aren't clamoring for glossy paper: According to *Garbage* Magazine, when the coating is removed from a ton of glossy paper, there's only a quarter to a half a ton of paper left.

• Nonetheless, recyclers are developing processes to make magazine recycling worth the effort. For example: Some recyclers are adding magazine scraps to their pulp to make their newsprint brighter.

WHY RECYCLE?

• We dump most of the magazines printed in the U.S. each year—about 8 million tons of them—into landfills. If we recycled just half of them, we could save over 12 million cubic yards of landfill space.

• That salvaged paper could be reprocessed into about 2 million tons of paperboard, the material cereal boxes are made of.

SIMPLE THINGS YOU CAN DO

1. Precycle

• Look over the magazines and catalogs you get. How many are unnecessarily printed on glossy stock? (Medical journals, for

In 1988, San Diego County expected 16,000 Christmas trees for recycling—and got 97,000.

example. Use your influence: Write to the publishers and suggest a change.

2. Reuse

• Give them to someone else to read. You can donate magazines to rest homes, or drop them off at schools for kids to cut up and use in class projects.

• Libraries sometimes appreciate getting magazines they don't subscribe to.

3. Find a Place to Recycle

• Your best bet is a recycling center, but the further you are from a major mill, the less likely it is that local recyclers will handle glossy paper.

• The reason: Because it's a low grade of paper, it may cost more to ship glossy stock than a recycler would receive in revenue. Remember, there's a bottom line to everybody's organization, even a nonprofit recycler's.

4. Recycle

• Don't mix magazines with any other paper unless your recycling center says it's okay.

• Keep glossy magazines separate from publications with newsprint pages—like phone books, Sears catalogs, *TV Guide*, etc. Newsprint is lower quality stock, and will downgrade the whole batch of recycled paper if it's included.

• Magazines with staples are fine; the staples are removed using screens during the recycling process. But magazines with glued bindings, such as *Reader's Digest* and *National Geographic*, can't be included yet; this is changing, however.

• Get rid of all plastic (if the magazine comes in a plastic wrapper or has an insert wrapped in plastic).

• Glossy junk mail is the same kind of paper as magazines, but isn't necessarily recyclable with them. Some mills find it too difficult to check every single piece of paper, so they restrict shipments to "magazines only." Check with your local recycler. You may have to recycle this with "mixed paper."

Currently, wax paper can't be recycled.

SACKS APPEAL

*In 1988, Americans used enough kraft paper for a person to take
a brown bag lunch to school or work for 64 million years.*

B ags are like newspapers—they keep accumulating, whether you want them or not. Every time you buy something, you get another bag. So you stash it in a closet or under the sink, and then go shopping again…and get some more bags.

You have an alternative: Reuse and recycle. If every household in the U.S. used old bags for just *one* grocery shopping trip, we might save as many as 60,000 trees.

IT'S IN THE BAG

• As much as 40% of the fiber used in paper bags can come from wood residue and waste paper. Some bags are being made with recycled corrugated cardboard.

SIMPLE THINGS YOU CAN DO

1. Precycle

• Think twice before taking a bag if your purchase is small.

• Bring your own mesh or cloth bags when you go shopping, as they do in Europe. They're available from many stores and catalogs.

• Ask your local grocer to stock bags made with recycled paper.

2. Reuse

• Many grocery stores will now pay up to 5¢ for each bag you bring back and reuse.

• Cut up brown bags and use them to wrap packages for mailing.

3. Recycle

• All brown paper bags can be recycled with corrugated cardboard. They're made of kraft paper, the same material as boxes.

• White and colored paper bags can be recycled with mixed paper.

FOR MORE INFORMATION

"The Paper Bag in Today's Environment." American Paper Institute, 260 Madison Ave., New York, NY 10016. (212) 340-0659.

Americans throw away around 10% of the food they buy at the supermarket.

PULP-POURRI

*Americans receive almost 4 million tons of junk mail
every year. Most of it winds up in landfills.*

L et's be honest about it; after you've recycled all the good
stuff—newspapers, magazines, and so on—you'll still have a
mountain of junk paper left over.

What do you do with those old egg cartons? The toilet paper
rolls? The old wrapping paper? You don't have to throw it all away.
Just toss odds and ends of paper into one bin, take the whole thing
to a recycling center and recycle it as "mixed paper."

MIX & MASH
• More and more "mixed paper" is junk mail. The latest stat: Every
man, woman and child in America gets about 248 pieces a year.

• There are so many contaminants in mixed paper—adhesives, for
example—that recycling it is an extremely messy job. The grade of
paper produced is lower, too.

WHY RECYCLE?
• It keeps millions of tons of paper out of landfills every year.

• Mixed paper can be made into boxboard—the thin, "cereal box"
type of cardboard. It's also made into roofing paper, tar paper and
asphalt shingles, and can be sorted into different grades, some with
higher values.

SIMPLE THINGS YOU CAN DO
1. Cut Your Scrap
• Make the most of your paper scraps: Cut them up and staple
them together to make note pads; reuse envelopes, etc.

• Stop your junk mail: Write to the Direct Marketing Association,
Attn: Mail Preference Service, 6 E. 43 St., New York, NY 10017.
Better yet, write to the companies that keep sending you mail.

2. See If Someone Will Take It
• Ask your local recycler if you're not sure. Most urban areas have
a facility that takes mixed paper. If you can't find one, try a roofing

Famous firsts: Curbside recycling originated in 1874 in Baltimore.

mill or building supply company.

Note: The further you live from a major mill, the harder it is to recycle mixed paper, because shipping to a mill isn't cost-effective.

3. Store It

• It's convenient to store mixed paper in a shopping bag. The bag is recyclable with the paper, so you won't have to empty it.

• Keep all plastic and string out of the mixed paper.

• Don't include: Fax paper, NCR paper (carbonless carbon paper), wax paper, paper towels, tissues, paper cups and plates.

4. Recycle

Junk Mail

• Before you recycle junk mail, open and sort through it to remove adhesive-backed stickers that will clog machines. (Even some environmental groups are sending them in the mail these days.)

• Glossy stock is okay. In fact, it's preferred by many mills.

• Envelopes with "lick-to-stick" or water soluble glue can be recycled, as long as you rip out plastic windows.

Paperboard

• Includes shoe boxes, cereal boxes, toilet paper rolls, cracker boxes, shirt cardboard, etc.

• Remove plastic or wax paper liners in cereal and cracker boxes.

• Crush all boxes to save space.

Egg Cartons, Berry Cartons, Paper Planters

• These are the lowest end of the recycling chain, and may already have been recycled. But they can still go to a paperboard mill.

• A little food waste is okay, but no eggshells.

Manila Envelopes

• No plastic bubble packs allowed.

• Some recyclers accept "post-its" and envelopes with adhesive labels attached, some don't. Check with your local recycling center.

• Metal clasps are okay—they're screened out. But before recycling, remove paper clips or binders for reuse.

Wrapping Paper

• Reuse it if you can. Otherwise, try to pull off most of the tape. (Little bits are okay). Remove string, ribbon and bows.

• No mylar or foil wrapping paper.

Paper saver: Use both sides of a sheet of paper whenever you can.

DIRECTORY ASSISTANCE

*The phone books from Phoenix, Arizona alone
generate 6,000 tons of wastepaper every year.*

Every year or so, a new set of phone books arrives on your doorstep. Wouldn't it be nice if you could recycle the old ones instead of dumping them in your garbage can?
Maybe you can. Some recycling centers accept phone books... And phone companies all over the U.S. are beginning to get the message that their customers want recycling.

DID YOU KNOW

• If Americans recycled their phone books for a year, we could save an estimated 650,000 tons of paper.

• If all our phone books were kept out of landfills, we could save some 2 million cubic yards of landfill space.

• Although phone books are made with the lowest possible quality paper, they can still be reprocessed and made into ceiling tiles, textbook covers, record album covers and insulation.

SIMPLE THINGS YOU CAN DO

1. Contact the Phone Company

• Ask if they recycle. If the company representative says they don't, suggest they start. Some companies claim it's not worth the effort, but if customers object, they could change their minds.

• Phone books aren't easy to recycle; the glue in the binding clogs papermaking machines. But some companies are now precycling, using easier-to-recycle glue, etc. Suggest it.

2. Find a Recycler

• Some recycling centers will take phone books with mixed paper.

• In some cases, if you rip out the pages, you can mix telephone books with newspapers. Check with your local recycling center.

Don't recycle Federal Express or UPS envelopes. They have plastic fiber in them.

PLASTIC

A PLASTIC WORLD

*Here are a few basic bits of info that might help
you make sense of of "plastics recycling."*

WHAT IS PLASTIC MADE OF?
A basic "batter" called resin, which is derived from oil or natural gas. Plastics makers buy resin from chemical companies, remelt it, and add chemicals. The hot liquid is molded under pressure, hardened and presto—it's a plastic container.

HOW MANY KINDS OF PLASTIC ARE THERE?
Almost 50 different kinds are used to make the things we use every day, like telephones, plumbing and packaging. The main types of plastic that consumers deal with are PET, HDPE, PVC, LDPE, Polypropylene and Polystyrene. We've included most of them here. In many cases, you can't tell one kind of plastic from another, so the plastics industry has introduced a coding system. Look on the bottom of each plastic container you buy for an imprinted recycling symbol with a number from 1-7 in the middle. Each number from 1-6 represents a different plastic; 7 means you can't recycle it.

ARE PLASTICS DANGEROUS TO MANUFACTURE?
The EPA has a laundry list of the chemicals that generate the most hazardous waste during production. The plastics industry uses 5 of the top 6 chemicals.

HOW ARE THEY RECYCLED?
The basic method: they're shredded into little flakes. The flakes are cleaned, dried, remelted—and formed into pellets to be used again.

CAN YOU RECYCLE A PLASTIC JUICE BOTTLE INTO ANOTHER ONE?
Technically yes, but a plastic food or drink container is unlikely to be recycled into another one because someone might have reused it to hold something less "appetizing," like motor oil. So recycled plastic, is usually "downgraded" into things that don't have to be sterile.

In 1988, Tucson, Arizona, collected 225 tons of phone books.

POP CULTURE

Americans go through 2.5 million plastic bottles every hour.

When people in the plastics industry talk about PET, they're not referring to Lassie or Mr. Ed. They're talking about *polyethylene terephthalate*.

You may not know the name, but you know the material. In fact, you may have some in your refrigerator right now; PET is what plastic soda bottles and peanut butter jars are made of.

Are you recycling it yet? Because of bottle bills around the country, one out of every four PET bottles are now recycled... and demand for the plastic currently exceeds supply. It's a good time to get started.

PET SOUNDS

• PET bottles account for most of the plastic currently being recycled in the U.S.

• PET bottles are actually a form of polyester. About a third of all the carpeting made in the U.S. has recycled PET bottles in it. Other uses: 26 recycled PET bottles equals a polyester suit; five recycled PET bottles make enough fiberfill to stuff a ski jacket.

• Recycling keeps around 175 million pounds of PET out of landfills every year. But 535 million pounds of PET are still being thrown away.

SIMPLE THINGS YOU CAN DO

1. Precycle

• If PET recycling isn't available in your community, consider buying glass bottles instead. Glass and aluminum recycling services are almost always available.

2. Find a Recycler

• In states with bottle bills, local markets or redemption centers are a good bet. In other states, give your local recyclers a call. If they don't accept PET, they'll know if anyone in your area does.

The average American can save six pounds of glass in a month.

• Check "Plastic Scrap" in the Yellow Pages. Or contact the National Association for Plastic Container Recovery (see below).

3. Open a PET Shop
• Store PET bottles with glass and cans. Many curbside programs take them together.

4. Identify It
• Look for the number in the recycling logo on the bottom of the container, inside the recycling sign. PET is #1.

• PET is usually clear (or clear green). Soda bottles are always PET, because it's the only plastic that can retain carbonation. Plastic liquor bottles are also always made of PET.

• Some products, like vegetable oil, are packed in either PET or PVC (*polyvinyl chloride*—see p. 64)containers. In the recycling process, a small amount of PVC can contaminate an entire batch of PET, so make sure you check the code.

• Other ways to tell the difference: On a PET container, there's a small raised dot or nipple—called a *gate*—in the center of the base. On a PVC container there's a straight seam, or a "smile," along the bottom. Also, PET bottles never have seams, PVC bottles do.

5. Prepare Bottles & Jars
• Rinse them lightly to keep them from attracting insects.

• Take off the tops, step on the bottles to flatten them (it makes handling and storage easier). If your state has a bottle bill, leave soft drink bottles intact; they're not redeemable if crushed.

• All PET containers can be recycled, including liquor and oil bottles, and peanut butter jars.

• In states with bottle bills, you can leave the caps on the bottles. Otherwise, recycle aluminum caps with aluminum cans; plastic caps are probably made of polypropylene, which is rarely recycled.

FOR MORE INFORMATION
"Pet Projects." A free newsletter from the National Association for Plastic Container Recovery (NAPCOR), 4828 Parkway Plaza Blvd., Suite 260, Charlotte, NC 28217;(800) 7-NAPCOR.

About 50% of the raw material for steel production comes from scrap.

THE JUG IS UP

*In case you wondered: **It takes 1,050 recycled
milk jugs to make a six foot plastic park bench.***

Milk jugs, butter tubs, detergent bottles, motor oil containers and bleach bottles are all made of a plastic called
high density polyethylene (HDPE, for short). It's tough, it's
lightweight, it's usually colorful…and it's all over the place; 62%
of all plastic bottles are made of the stuff.

Americans have been using more and more HDPE every year,
but manufacturers never made much of an effort to recycle it.
Now, with landfill space at a premium and consumers taking a
hard look at packaging materials, the plastics industry has begun
to develop recycling programs.

If we're not going to stop using HDPE, it only makes sense that
we should be recycling it.

SHALL WE DENSE?

• Recycled HDPE can be turned into items like flowerpots, trash
cans, traffic barrier cones and curbside recycling bins.

• In 1988 we used 2 billion pounds of HDPE just to make bottles
for household products. That's about the weight of 900,000
Honda Civics.

• If every American household recycled just one out of every ten
HDPE bottles they used, we'd keep 200 million pounds of the
plastic out of landfills every year.

• Some detergent bottles are already being made with 30% recycled HDPE. The only drawback: There's no way to control the
color of recycled plastic, so it's sandwiched between layers of
colorful new virgin plastic.

• According to experts, clean HDPE scrap can be worth $150-
600 a ton. At $150 a ton, we discard as much as $120 million
worth of it every year.

The landfill gas produced daily at Fresh Kills Landfill is enough fuel to heat 50,000 homes.

SIMPLE THINGS YOU CAN DO

1. Precycle

• If there's no way to recycle HDPE in your area, consider buying products that don't come in plastic bottles. Sample alternatives: Detergent in a recycled box, milk in refillable bottles (which are starting to reappear in supermarkets).

• Buy large containers whenever you can.

• Reuse HDPE containers whenever possible. Mark them clearly to cut down on "refrigerator mysteries." For safety, don't put dangerous liquids in food containers.

2. Look for a Recycler

• The number of plastics recyclers is increasing, so you may be able to find one that accepts most rigid containers.
• If nothing's readily available, try looking in the Yellow Pages under "Plastics, Used."

3. Identify It

• Check the bottom of the container. If it has a #2 inside the recycling logo, it's HDPE.

• Without the recycling code, it's tough to tell what is HDPE and what is polypropylene. If there's no code, tell the store manager or manufacturer you want clear labeling.

• Yogurt or cottage cheese containers, for example, could be either material—or polystyrene. Ask local recyclers what types of plastics they accept, and for tips on telling the difference between them.

• Plastic bags are made out of both HDPE and LDPE. It's easy to tell the difference: LDPE bags are slightly waxy to the touch, stretch easily, and are "quieter." HDPE bags make a crinkly noise.

4. Recycle

• Remove the caps. These are almost always polypropylene—essentially non-recyclable right now. Throw the "collars" away.

• Rinse the containers (plastic retains the smell of sour milk). Stomp on them to flatten them and conserve storage space.

• Some recyclers want labels taken off. Check with them.

Ben and Jerry's ice cream recycles 100,000 five-gallon HDPE containers every year.

VINYL EXAM

How long does it take for vinyl to decompose in a landfill?
According to Save Our Planet, *"as many as four centuries."*

D o you know where your vinyl is?
You walk on it. You use it to water your lawn. You even buy dinner with it.

Technically, it's called *polyvinyl chloride*, or PVC. It's used to make bottles (water, shampoo, cooking oil), garden hoses, flooring, credit cards, shower curtains and much more. About 5% of all plastic packaging is PVC.

It can be recycled—but it rarely is.

WHY RECYCLE?

• We produce more than 8 billion pounds of PVC annually. But only 500,000-600,000 pounds of it is recycled.

• In landfills: If certain PVC containers are exposed to water, solvents, or other trash, "plasticizers"—chemicals added to make the plastic more flexible—can leach into water and soil.

• In incinerators: PVC contains chlorinated compounds. When it's incinerated with other trash, it releases hydrochloric acid, a corrosive. Some experts believe it also releases toxic, cancer-causing dioxins.

...AND THAT'S VINYL

• The jury is still out on whether PVC is safe for packaging food.

• In 1975, a carcinogen called vinyl chloride monomer was found to be leaching into liquor from PVC bottles.

• Manufacturers say they've solved the problem, but if you look around, you won't see many foods in PVC containers (due to the threat of lawsuits).

• An exception: Some experts say that film with PVC in it—used with cheese, lunch meats, franks, bacon, etc.—is a superior packaging material for perishables. Hazards are probably minimal.

In 1987, Americans earned over $100 million recycling cardboard boxes.

• However, certain brands of bottled water are packaged in PVC containers. The Environmental Defense Fund suggests that you buy bottled water in glass or PET containers instead. Look on the bottom of your water bottle to check the material before you buy.

SIMPLE THINGS YOU CAN DO

1. Precycle

• If there's no way to recycle PVC in your area, consider buying products made of other materials. Sample alternatives: Water or cooking oil in glass—rather than plastic—bottles.

2. Find a Place to Take It

• Not so simple, really; PVC isn't easy to recycle yet. Call a local recycling center to ask if they know a place that accepts it.
• Try the Vinyl Institute, Wayne Interchange Plaza II, 155 Rte. 45 West, Wayne, NJ 07470. It's a manufacturers' trade organization.

3. Pick Out PVC

• The recycling code on PVC products is #3, and there should be the letter "V" for vinyl.

• PVC is usually shiny and tough. One way to identify it (but destroy it): It's PVC if a white crease appears when you bend it (like credit cards).

• Clear bottles with a slightly blue tint (e.g., some imported mineral waters) are PVC.

• Any clear, colorless bottles that aren't PET are probably PVC.

4. Recycle

• Take off the bottle caps. They're probably polypropylene.

• Rinse the bottles and flatten them.

• It's important to keep all PVC separate from other types of plastic when you're recycling bottles. A little PVC can ruin an entire batch of recycled plastic—as well as machinery—if it gets mixed up with PET.
• The reason: According to plastics recyclers, if it gets too hot, PVC can turn into hydrochloric acid and eat away the chrome on the recycling equipment.

In 1988, Americans recycled about 1 million tons of stainless steel.

WRAP MUSIC

*Every year, we make enough plastic film
to shrink-wrap the state of Texas.*

Here's a quiz. Which of these items are made of *low-density polyethylene* (LDPE, for short)? It doesn't matter if you've never heard of the stuff—take a guess anyway.

A) The shrink wrap packaging on cassettes and CDs, B) plastic sandwich bags, C) the plastic cover that protects your dry-cleaning.

The answer is: All of them.

This thin, "filmy" substance is the leader in the plastic packaging parade. Every year we use almost 5 million tons—9.5 *billion pounds*—of it. And how much is currently recycled? As *Garbage* Magazine puts it politely, "Amount recycled: Negligible."

WHY RECYCLE?

• Plastic bags and film wrappings account for 40% of our plastic garbage. Most of it's going to be sitting in landfills for centuries.

• There's no evidence yet that "biodegradable" plastic bags safely degrade in landfills. At best, the bags break into invisible—and probably toxic—little chips. So recycling is a better option.

• Theoretically, the more LDPE we recycle, the less we'll need to produce. That means less oil and natural gas used, and fewer chemicals like benzene produced in manufacturing it.

• Plastic bags are among the few plastic products that may be recycled in a closed loop—i.e., recycled plastic bags are made into more plastic bags.

SIMPLE THINGS YOU CAN DO

1. Precycle

• As Jeanne Wirka says in *Wrapped In Plastic*, "It's common sense: The most efficient way to deal with the waste problem is to produce less waste to begin with." Most LDPE comes into our lives as disposable packaging.

The number of yard waste composting programs increased by over 50% in 1989.

• This applies to plastic bags, too. Before taking them in supermarkets, for example, consider whether you really need them. Can you leave your vegetables loose? Have you tried bundling carrots, etc. with rubber bands?

• If you can, take dry cleaning without the plastic covering.

• Once you've got plastic bags at home, reuse them. If necessary, they can be washed. Rinse them, turn them inside out, and hang them on a clothesline to dry. Why recycle when you can reuse?

2. Find a Place to Take It

• Manufacturers are working with supermarkets to set up in-store LDPE plastic bag recycling. Check with your local supermarket to see if they have a program for recycling plastic bags. Find out if the bags will actually be recycled.

• Call a local recycling center.

3. Identify It

• Check plastic bags for the recycling code. There will be a #4 inside the recycling symbol if it's LDPE. If there's no symbol, it's probably LDPE anyway.

• LDPE is also in plastic film around building products, shipping crates and most soft plastic grocery bags.

• How do you tell if a grocery bag is LDPE? It doesn't make noise when you crinkle it.

DON'Ts

• "Cling" wrap isn't LDPE. The ingredient that makes it stick, called a "tackifier," makes it a lower grade of film. Don't recycle it with your LDPE.

• Don't recycle cellophane with LDPE—it's made of wood fiber.

• Don't recycle potato chip bags and candy wrappers with LDPE. They're made of polypropylene film.

• Don't recycle foil / plastic laminates.

• **Note:** If you're recycling bags, make sure they're clean and dry.

Only 5% of U.S. residents take their hazardous products to designated collection sites.

PUT A LID ON IT

Of the almost 3.2 billion pounds of polypropylene used for packaging in 1988, 98% of it was thrown away.

Polypropylene is used to make the little things we hardly notice—plastic bottle caps, plastic lids, drinking straws, broom fibers, rope, twine, yogurt containers and carpet.
So why bother mentioning it? Because Americans use over 3.5 million tons of it every year...And so far, only about 1% of it is being recycled. This is something we need to change.

TO CAP IT OFF...

• Polypropylene is "the lightest of the major plastics." Over half of it goes into packaging.

• Theoretically, recycling will reduce the amount of new polypropylene manufactured. That's a positive step, because the chemical *propylene* is at the very top of the EPA's list of "worst toxics."

• When polypropylene is incinerated, it gives off nickel, a very toxic metal which has been found to increase incidences of lung and nose cancer.

SIMPLE THINGS YOU CAN DO

1. Find a Recycler

• Good luck. Although it's technically recyclable, the plastics industry has made little effort to start polypropylene recycling programs. If you find a recycling center that takes this plastic, ask for details on how to prepare it.

2. Identify It

• If a recycling center near you accepts polypropylene, look for the #5 in the recycling logo on container bottoms.

• Polypropylene is usually opaque. Practically all plastic bottle caps and lids are made with it.

• You'll also find it in: syrup bottles, some yogurt containers and cottage cheese tubs, battery casings, disposable diaper linings.

It takes half a barrel of crude oil to produce the rubber in just one truck tire.

HOLD THE FOAM

Every year, Americans use more than
25 billion polystyrene foam cups.

H ave you ever thought about recycling a Styrofoam cup? Hard to imagine, isn't it? By the time you're done with one, chances are you've crumbled it up, poked holes in it, or taken a bite out of it.

The fact is, you can't *get* more disposable than polystyrene foam. And yet, the plastics industry has set up pilot recycling programs to demonstrate that it can be turned into things like light switch plates, note pad holders, and cassette tape boxes. Amazing.

Now environmentalists, concerned citizens, and plastics manufacturers are engaged in a debate about whether polystyrene foam is worth collecting and transporting for recycling...or whether it should just be phased out altogether.

FOAM AGAIN, FOAM AGAIN

• How are fast food containers recycled? They're dumped into a tub of water, then sprayed through a screen that breaks them into pieces. These are washed, dried, melted and turned into pellets—which are sold to a manufacturer, who makes them into new items.
• Polystyrene isn't just used to make foam; you'll find it in some containers, too (like yogurt tubs). They have a #6 on the bottom.

WHY RECYCLE?

• Polystyrene foam is completely non-biodegradable. It just won't go away. Even 500 years from now, the foam coffee cup you used this morning will be sitting in a landfill.

• Foam that doesn't get buried or burned winds up in the ocean, where it endangers animals like turtles, who mistake it for food.

• Polystyrene foam is made from benzene, a known carcinogen. It's converted to styrene, and then injected with gases to make it a foam product. The gases are either pentane (which contributes to smog) or HCFC-22 (which contributes to ozone layer destruction).

In 1989, America used about 14 million tons of newsprint.

SIMPLE THINGS YOU CAN DO

1. Precycle

• Recycling foam products isn't like recycling glass—we don't make new cups or plates from old ones—so recycling won't cut down the amount of virgin materials used to make the millions of new cups and other items we use every day...or the pollution.

• It's probably better to find a reusable substitute. For example: Bring a coffee cup to work instead of using disposable foam ones.

2. Reuse

• Don't recycle foam packing "peanuts" or throw them away. Reuse them instead. Include a note in the package suggesting the next person reuse them, too.

• If you don't want to reuse them, take them to a store that can.

• Tell the company that sent the peanuts to you not to use them.

3. Find a Recycler

• Not so simple, really. Most of the recycling focus is on collecting polystyrene foam from businesses. Practically speaking, there *is* no place for individuals to take it yet.

• One reason: There aren't many facilities to process it. According to EDF, as of mid-1990, only four plants in the U.S. were recycling post-consumer polystyrene...and one barely worked.

• Another reason: People usually take "carry-out" containers away from restaurants or stores—so there probably won't be a foam recycling bin around when they're ready to throw the foam away.

• To find out if you can recycle foam in your area, contact the Polystyrene Packaging Institute. Ask them for recycling details.

FOR MORE INFORMATION

Pro-Foam: "Polystyrene—Recycle It!" The Polystyrene Packaging Institute, 1025 Connecticut Ave NW, Suite 513, Washington, D.C. 20036. *This is a manufacturers' trade group.*

Anti-Foam: Local Solutions to Global Pollution, 2121 Bonar St., Berkeley, CA 94702. *For information, send a self-addressed, stamped envelope.*

The largest component of trash in landfills is newspapers (14% by volume).

ORGANICS

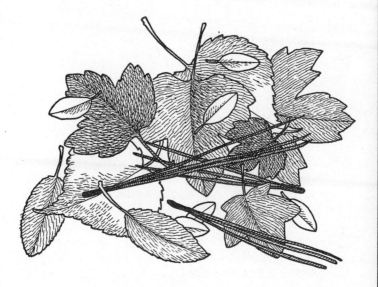

IT'S ONLY NATURAL

What is all this garbage?

WHAT IS COMPOSTING?
It's the process of letting living organisms "eat" organic material and turn it into a rich, crumbly soil called *humus*.
- Nature is one giant composting system. For example, when leaves fall, they rot, then get eaten up by bacteria...and eventually become enriched soil which helps new plants get started.
- You can do composting, too. It's not difficult: you keep a bin outside (or just a pile) of organic material, then put your food and yard waste on it.

HOW DOES IT WORK?
Basically, you put down layers of dry stuff, like straw, then wet stuff, like food. You mix the pile every few days so air can circulate, and you add water to keep it damp.
- How long does it take to "compost?" About 1-4 months.
- Note: You don't necessarily have to stir the pile, but the process will take longer (6 months to a year).
- We're not trying to be definitive in this section. Composting is a complex science...maybe even an art, and although we encourage you to get involved, we recommend you check out the resources we've suggested before taking the first step.

WHAT CAN YOU COMPOST?
You can't put everything in compost—some things, for example, pet waste, add organisms that could carry disease. The San Francisco Recycling Program also advise not to compost meat, bones, fat or grease; these take too long to break down, stink, and attract pests.

ARE PEOPLE REALLY GOING TO COMPOST?
It does take a little effort. But the rewards are worth it: great fertilizer for your garden and the satisfaction of saving landfill space.
- If having a compost pile in your yard isn't for you, don't worry, there's an alternative; municipal composting sites or community gardens where you can take yard waste. (They'll probably charge you less than it costs to dispose of yard waste in a landfill, too.)

There are a billion organisms in every gram of compost.

TURN OVER AN OLD LEAF

There are 20 million acres of grass in the U.S.—the equivalent of a lawn as big as the states of Vermont, New Hampshire, Massachusetts and Rhode Island...combined.

I f you're like most of us, the main thing on your mind when you mow grass or rake leaves is, "How long will this take?"

The last thing you're concerned about is the long-term effect of dumping all that waste into your local landfill. After all, it's organic material, right?

Yes...But that's a good reason to *recycle* it, not throw it away. Yard waste isn't garbage—it can be used as compost, mulch or in some instances, even fuel. So why pay to dump it?

WHY RECYCLE?

• Americans throw away 28 million tons of mowed grass, dead leaves and branches every year—almost 20% of all our solid waste.

• According to *Complete Trash*, grass makes up 70% of all yard waste. (The amount varies by region). That's remarkable, because grass doesn't even need to be picked up—if the clippings are short enough, they will quickly decompose and supply the soil with nitrogen and carbon.

• Fallen leaves contain 50-80% of the nutrients that a tree extracts from the earth. By composting them, we're helping the earth replenish itself.

• When seemingly "safe" yard waste is buried in landfills—where there isn't much oxygen—it releases explosive methane gas, a powerful "greenhouse gas" that contributes to air pollution and global warming. Methane and other toxics can also condense into liquid and leach into groundwater.

• Recycling an average-size family's yard waste can make about 300-400 pounds of finished compost, or *humus*, a year.

Plastics make up about 7% of America's garbage.

SIMPLE THINGS YOU CAN DO

1. Find a Place to Take It

• Your own yard is the best place. Even if you don't have a formal compost pile, you can compost some yard waste.

• To find other alternatives: Call a local recycling center. If they can't accept it, they'll know who can. Local environmental groups are also likely to know something about composting in your area.

• Call your public works department to find out if your community has municipal composting. Find out about collection and drop-offs.

2. Simple Strategies

• The easiest way to recycle grass: "Cut it high, let it lie." Keep grass at 2-3", taking off a little at a time. In a few days, short clippings disappear between the blades and naturally fertilize the lawn. This technique is also useful during droughts; it keeps soil cooler and wetter.

• You can rake the grass into a pile in the corner of your yard. It's not a great solution—moist grass takes a month or two to decompose—but it's better than dumping it into a landfill.

• You can rake leaves into a pile, too. They also take a little while to break down, but again, it's better than landfilling them.

• Whole leaves can be spread around woodland areas or on the ground under hardy plants and shrubs. If you want to spread them on a garden, add some extra nitrogen.

• Large pieces of wood, 3" in diameter or more, make good firewood when they're dried.

3. Use a Compost Pile

• It's the simplest, most efficient way to recycle yard waste.

• For grass: If you're using a standard mower, take the bag full of grass clippings and add it to your compost pile. Add the grass in thin layers, so it doesn't compact.

• Add leaves to a compost pile...or surround them with chicken wire and use them to start a compost pile.

We recycle about 20% of the plastic soda bottles we use.

4. Get Some Equipment

• Wood must be run through a "chipper" to be recycled. The chips can be used as a mulch or spread on walkways, play areas, etc. You can get a household chipper, but most can only handle branches about 3" in diameter. Look in the Yellow Pages under "Tree Services" for bigger ones.

• If you're buying a new lawnmower, consider a "mulching" type. It chops grass into very fine pieces and dumps it back onto the lawn.

• If you have a shredder, run leaves through it. It will speed the composting time. If you don't have one, contact a landscaper or gardener who does...Or consider buying one jointly with your neighbors.

FOR MORE INFORMATION

• **"E.A.S.Y Lawn Mowing."** Colorado State Cooperative Extension, 1700 S. Holly, Denver, Colorado, 80222, (303) 692-5600. *Free tips on keeping your lawn healthy, cutting trash disposal costs.*

• **"Home Composting."** Seattle Tilth Association, 4649 Sunnyside Ave. N., Seattle, WA 98103. *A "how-to" brochure; send $2.50 (plus .50 postage) and a SASE.*

• **The Rodale Guide to Composting.** By J. Minnich (Rodale Press, 1979).

• **Worms Eat My Garbage.** By M. Appelhoff (Flower Press, 1982). *A fascinating, easy-to-read guide to worm composting.*

COMPOST BINS

Here are a few mail order catalogs that sell compost bins.

• **Gardens Alive,** P.O. Box 149, Sunman, IN 47041. (812) 623-3800.

• **Gardener's Supply,** Dept. PR-91. 128 Intervale Rd., Burlington, VT 05401. (802) 863-1700.

• **7th Generation,** Colchester, VT 05446-1672. (800) 456-1177.

Trash tip: Putting old tires around tomato plants can help them grow faster.

LEFTOVERS AGAIN?

Americans dump the equivalent of more than 21 million shopping bags full of food into landfills every year.

When you were young, did your parents make you eat everything on your plate? Now that you're a grown-up, you don't have to. But what happens to those leftovers? One expert estimates that Americans throw away more than 870,000 pounds of food every day.

There's an alternative: Composting will turn practically any food into natural fertilizer. If we compost food scraps (except meat, which will attract insects and animal pests to your backyard) instead of dumping them into the garbage, they'll nourish the soil as they decompose. And practically anyone can have a compost pile...or take part in a municipal composting program.

WHY RECYCLE?

• Food waste currently makes up an astounding 8% to 12% of the garbage we send to landfills. That's around 320 million pounds of leftover food every year.

• A sink disposal isn't the answer. It shreds food waste and sends it to the wastewater treatment plant in your area. It comes out as sludge, another huge disposal problem. And even if the sludge is composted, it has restricted uses because it may be contaminated by other waste.

• Food adds nitrogen to a compost pile, which speeds up the composting process and helps make better fertilizer.

SIMPLE THINGS YOU CAN DO

1. Give It Away

• Most communities have food banks or homeless shelters. They always need food. If you have a lot of extra fresh food, consider donating it to them.

2. Find a Place to Put It

• Start your own compost pile, or find a neighbor who's got one.

Since Massachusetts passed its bottle bill, emergency rooms report 60% fewer glass-related cuts.

- Call your public works department to find out if there's municipal composting in your community.

2. Set Up

- Keep a large yogurt-type container (holds about a quart) by your sink or cutting board.
- Some people also keep a large container—like a five-gallon plastic bucket or garbage pail with a tight-fitting lid (to keep odors from escaping)—in the kitchen, under the sink or wherever there is room.

3. Compost Your Food

- Put food scraps in the yogurt container while you're fixing meals.
- Whenever the yogurt container is full, dump it into the larger container...or take it out directly to the compost pile.
- The lid on the large container keeps the smell inside; open it as little as possible.
- Other ways to keep the smell from becoming a problem: Empty it frequently. And try sprinkling sawdust on top of food. It's like compost "kitty litter," absorbing and masking odors. Need sawdust? Most lumber yards gladly give it to you for free.
- Take food scraps from your bucket to the compost pile regularly and mix it in thoroughly.
- Remember: To avoid bees and flies, always cover kitchen scraps with a layer of leaves, grass or dirt.

FOR MORE INFORMATION

- **"The Simple Art of Home Composting."** Ecology Action, P.O. Box 1188, Santa Cruz, CA 95061; (408) 476-8088. *Easy-to-read guide; $3.*
- ***Organic Gardening* Magazine,** Rodale Press, E. Minor St., Emmaus, PA 18098-0015; (800) 441-7761. *The monthly source for organic gardeners; $16.97/year.*
- ***Let It Rot: The Gardener's Guide to Composting,*** Story Communications, Schoolhouse Rd., Pownal, VT 05261; (802) 823-5811. *The ultimate "how-to" compost book; $11.70.*

Metals make up 9% of all municipal solid waste (by weight).

YULE RECYCLE

Every year, the U.S. and Canada chop down 34 million Christmas trees—enough to cover the state of Rhode Island with a forest.

When the holidays are over and the ornaments are all back in the boxes, what do you do with your tree? What *can* you do except throw it away?

How about recycling it? Lots of communities have successful recycling programs. They collect the trees and run them through "chippers" that turn them into mulch—a present for plants.

TREE'S A CROWD

• Over 100 U.S. communities currently recycle Christmas trees. San Diego, California, started the trend in 1971. In 1989, the city recycled close to 100,000 trees (both cut and live).

• In a supervised project, Boulder County, Colorado dumped over 5,000 old Christmas trees on the bottoms of nearby lakes. Sound strange? It's an ecological benefit—the trees shelter fish and attract bugs for them to eat.

SIMPLE THINGS YOU CAN DO

1. Precycle

Try a living Christmas tree. Buy a tree in a pot, and plant it after Christmas. Talk to people at a local nursery to find out how.

2. Find a Place to Take It

Call your public works or sanitation departments to find out if your community has a program for recycling Christmas trees. (Some towns just collect and dump them). If not, suggest they start one.

3. Recycle

• Clean the tree—remove tinsel, ornaments and lights. (Believe it or not, people sometimes even forget to take off the stands.) If non-organic items are left on the tree, the mulch will be contaminated by metal or plastic chips.

• You'll probably need to drop it off at a specially designated location. But the tree will have dried out and gotten lighter, so it will be easier to carry than when you bought it.

OTHER

RECYCLABLES

RAG-TIME

In 1988, America exported 135,000 tons of
used clothing to Third World countries.

N o, clothes can't be recycled the way bottles and cans are recycled. You can't melt down an old pair of bellbottoms and come up with new blue jeans.

But old clothes can be reused. By donating them to nonprofit organizations like Goodwill Industries or the Salvation Army, you provide clothes for disaster victims and the homeless, and redistribute them into your community through nonprofit thrift stores.

Second-hand clothes are also important to people in Third World countries. Americans send millions of tons of old clothing to Africa and Asia every year. In 1988, for example, 23 million pounds of used textiles went to Pakistan alone. In fact, someone there may be wearing your old blouse or sports shirt right now.

CASE CLOTHED

• About 835,000 pairs of jeans are produced in the U.S. every day.

• It's hard to reuse most fabrics to make new clothes because they're treated with chemicals, or "finished" to make them smooth, or they've been chemically combined with other fabrics.

• However, wool is occasionally recycled that way. It has long fibers which can be pulled apart and rewoven. And cotton fibers are sometimes recycled into high quality paper.

WHY RECYCLE?

• It saves resources. About half the clothes Americans wear are made of synthetic fibers produced from oil—a non-renewable resource.

• The rest are made of natural fibers like cotton, often produced with pesticides, chemical fertilizers, etc. Making them has already had an effect on the earth; we owe it to the planet to use them as long as they last.

• Reusing clothes can save landfill space, too; in Washington

D.C., for example, 2 million pounds of clothes are kept out of landfills every year by the Salvation Army alone.

SIMPLE THINGS YOU CAN DO

1. Find a Place to Recycle

• Call Goodwill Industries, the Salvation Army, the St. Vincent DePaul Society, or a similar organization. Ask for information on the nearest drop-off locations in your area.

• To find the number, look in the Yellow Pages under "Clothing, Used," or "Second-hand."

• Alternative: Donate clothes to a local homeless shelter or charity. Look in the Yellow Pages under "Charitable Organizations."

2. Do a Little Quality Control Before Donating

• Wash the clothes first. It saves a thrift store time and money.

• Try to pick out clothes that are in good shape—no tears, major stains, or missing zippers.

• Unwearable cotton clothes are often still accepted—they're shipped overseas or used as rags. But most organizations would rather not have to deal with them.

• Buttons missing? No problem. Clothes are priced accordingly.

3. Recycle

• The most efficient way to recycle your clothes is to donate them in season. If you pass on unwanted sweaters at the beginning of winter, for example, they'll be on the racks at thrift stores when they're most needed—and the organizations won't have to store them till next year.

• Don't use a thrift store as a "garbage dump." It costs them money. Goodwill Industries, for example, already has an annual garbage bill of well over $1 million. They have other things they'd rather do with the money.

• Recycle at home: Make rags out of old shirts, etc. Use them in the kitchen and bathroom instead of relying on disposable towels.

There are only 23 permanent household hazardous waste collection sites in the U.S.

GET THE LEAD OUT

*Sixty percent of the world's lead supply
comes from recycled car batteries.*

Here's a riddle: What's a foot long, is sitting in your car, and has about 20 pounds of poison in it?

Want a hint? You probably never think of it unless your car won't start.

Yes, it's your car battery, which contains 18 pounds of toxic lead, and a gallon of sulfuric acid—two hazardous wastes you don't want to dump into the environment.

Fortunately, you can take a car battery to a gas station or auto parts store, and they'll recycle it for you.

RE-VOLTING!

• Americans recycle about 80 percent of our car batteries. But the other 20 percent—containing about 330 million pounds of lead—wind up in landfills.

• How are batteries recycled? Companies called "battery breakers" crack each one open and drain out the sulfuric acid (which is either reprocessed or sent to a hazardous waste facility). Then the batteries go to a scrap yard. The lead is removed and shipped to a mill, where it's melted down into ingots. It's sold to manufacturers …and might very well end up in your new car battery. The polypropylene case is also recycled.

• Recycling only Minnesota's used car batteries for a year would keep 7.6 million pounds of lead and 400,000 gallons of sulfuric acid out of landfills.

WHY RECYCLE?

• It's estimated that three out of every four Americans who change their own car batteries throw them away instead of recycling. In landfills, battery cases eventually crack, allowing the lead and acid to pollute groundwater.

A paper grocery sack holds about 1.5 lbs. of empty aluminum cans.

- Lead is poisonous. It can cause liver, kidney and brain damage. About 250,000 children suffer from lead poisoning each year.
- Car batteries contribute 2/3 of all lead in municipal waste.
- Incinerating batteries spews lead into the air.

SIMPLE THINGS YOU CAN DO

If a Service Station Changes Your Battery

- Check first to make sure they plan to recycle it. If not, take your business somewhere else.

If You Replace Your Own Battery
1. Precycle

- Buy the new battery from someone who'll take the old one as a trade in, and can guarantee it will be recycled. Usually retailers who sell batteries—auto parts stores, local gas stations, etc.—gather battery casings and recycle in volume.

2. Handle With Care

- Battery acid sometimes leaks. The fumes are dangerous; they can seriously irritate your eyes. And the liquid can eat away clothes and burn your skin. Wear gloves.

3. Recycle Right Away

- Apparently, people aren't aware of the health and safety risks involved with battery storage.
- The proof: In a recent study, the EPA found that one-fourth of the people who change their own batteries have at least *six* of them in their garages.
- If you've got a bunch of batteries stashed away and a service station or other retailer won't take them, call the local household hazardous waste facility. (Ask your municipal government for the location.)

By 1915, 89% of all major U.S. cities had municipal garbage collection service.

DEADLY DO-RIGHT

*Every day, American families produce an estimated
4 million pounds of household hazardous waste.*

Who's dumping hazardous waste into the environment? It's not just factories—you could be doing it, too. As much as 25% of America's hazardous waste comes from private homes.

Take a look around—is there any coming from your house?

Here's a help: According to the National Association of Solvent Recyclers, hazardous household waste includes:

- Spot Remover
- Lighter Fluid
- Paint Stripper
- Pesticides
- Furniture Polish
- Nail Polish
- Nail Polish Remover
- Drain Openers
- Scouring Powders
- Oven Cleaners
- Toilet Bowl Cleaner
- Adhesives, like "Super Glue"
- Caulk
- Paints and Thinners
- Mothballs

The best solution is to use as little of these products as possible, but recycling is a limited alternative. And some can be passed on to neighbors and friends who'll use them up—which is certainly better than throwing them away.

RECYCLING FACTS

• According to *Garbage* magazine, each family in the U.S. produces about 15 pounds of hazardous waste a year.

• It's practical to recycle certain hazardous materials in large quantities. Cleaners like spot remover, for example, can be reprocessed and reconstituted by cleaning them up—if there's a large amount.

There are 40 facilities in the U.S. which recover landfill gas.

- Solvents can be re-refined together; the residue from recycling them can be burned as a "backup" fuel. Hazardous waste facilities collect solvents and ship them to factories for reprocessing.

- In 1989, 400 million gallons of solvents, the equivalent of 800,000 tons of coal—were burned as fuel.

WHY RECYCLE?

- If you throw hazardous waste into the trash instead of recycling it, you may injure a garbage collector. According to one study, 3% of California's collectors were hurt by handling hazardous items that shouldn't have been tossed out in the first place.

- If just 1% of American families cut their hazardous waste in half, we'd keep 7.3 million pounds of it out of our landfills and waterways. And if just 10% of us cut our hazardous waste in half, we'd keep 73 million pounds of the stuff out of the Earth.

- When you pour hazardous waste down the drain, it goes untreated into lakes, rivers and streams, because most municipal sewage plants aren't set up to purify it.

- Some household wastes in landfills are so potent that they eat through steel and plastic containers.

- Once they're out, they can seep unnoticed into water supplies; only one out of every four U.S. landfills actually monitors groundwater. Even worse: 95% of the landfills would have no way to collect toxic leachate even if they detected it.

SIMPLE THINGS YOU CAN DO

1. Precycle

- Use safe alternatives whenever possible. "Green" consumer products are increasingly available in supermarkets and hardware stores.

- You can make your own alternatives—for example, ovens can be cleaned with baking soda and steel wool. Books like *Nontoxic, Natural, & EarthWise* (see next page) are full of suggestions.

- Dry cleaning solvents can be reprocessed and distilled. (There are even small recycling machines a dry cleaner can buy and use on location.) Choose a dry cleaner who will guarantee that his or her solvents are recycled.

Employees at financial businesses generate about 2 lbs. of paper a day...per person!

2. Store Them

• Keep them in a cool, protected area, out of the sunlight.

• Store and label them properly.

• Keep them in the original containers, with labels intact. If a label falls off, replace it with another, more permanent one. Materials can't be reused or recycled if you're not sure what they are.

• If the container starts to leak, put the whole thing in a larger container and label both containers well.

3. Find a Place to Take Them

• Some communities have "waste exchanges" or "drop & swap" exchanges where people trade usable portions of hazardous products. Call your municipal government to see if there's one near you. If not, consider starting one.

• Pass them on to neighbors who'll use them up.

• Call your municipal government and see about taking products to a household hazardous waste facility. Ask if there's a hazardous waste "collection day" in your community. If not, tell them to start one!

4. Recycle

• If you're taking it to a hazardous waste center, consider making it a neighborhood effort.

• The only drawback: There are usually limitations on how much one person is allowed to bring to a center. Before picking up waste, check to see how much you're allowed to bring in your car.

FOR MORE INFORMATION

• **Nontoxic, Natural, & Earthwise.** By Debra Lynn Dadd. Published by Jeremy Tarcher. *Hundreds of alternatives to household toxics.*

• **Once Is Not Enough: A Citizen's Recycling Manual.** National Toxics Campaign, 1168 Commonwealth Ave., Boston, MA, 02134; (617) 232-0327. *Outlines solid waste issues, tips for organizing local recycling. $4.50.*

• **"Household Hazardous Waste News,"** Dana Duxbury and Associates, Waste Watch Center, 16 Haverhill Street, Andover, MA 01810. (508) 470-3044. *Free quarterly newsletter.*

Virtually 100% of car batteries returned to gas stations and battery dealerships get recycled.

COOL AID

*In 1988, Americans dumped over 21 million pounds
of antifreeze into the environment.*

Who cares about old antifeeze? You probably would, if you knew it was polluting your water supply.

Well it is. For years, we've routinely dumped antifreeze in sewers or on the ground. Now we've discovered that it's toxic…so service stations are beginning to recycle it.

THE COLD FACTS
• Antifreeze has been designated a hazardous waste by the state of California. Other states are expected to do the same soon.

• Most antifreeze is made with a petroleum product called ethylene glycol. It's a hazard to pets as well as the environment—they're attracted to puddles of it by its sweet taste; they drink it and die.

• There are two ways to recycle antifreeze. The most effective and reliable is to have it re-distilled.

• The alternative: A machine is used to filter out contaminants. New antifreeze is then added to bring the old liquid up to full-strength. This method is apparently questionable, as several car manufacturers will not honor it for their warranties.

SIMPLE THINGS YOU CAN DO
If a Service Station Changes Your Antifreeze
• Make sure they intend to send the old stuff out to be recycled. If they don't, take your business elsewhere…and tell them why.

If You Change It Yourself
• Drain it into a clean container with a tight-fitting lid.

• Find a place to take it. First choice: Service stations or automotive repair shops. But remember: They pay to have their antifreeze taken away and recycled, so you may have to pay a fee.

Note: If antifreeze is designated a hazardous waste in your area, service stations may not accept it. But hazardous waste facilities often stockpile antifreeze and recycle it periodically. Call to find out.

A cubic yard of newspaper weighs about 600 lbs.

EDIFICE WRECKS

*Americans hammer down 400 acres' worth
of asphalt roofing each day.*

A re you remodeling your home, or building a new one? Here's something you may not have figured into your costs: Disposing of old 2 x 4's, sheetrock, etc. costs a lot of money. But you can reduce expenses and do your part to help keep millions of tons of building waste out of our landfills by reusing and recycling it instead.

CONSTRUCTIVE COMMENTS

• In Colonial times, nails were so precious that before settlers moved West, they burned down their houses to reclaim the nails.

• In 1989, we spent $92 billion renovating and remodeling homes. In fact, we spend more money on renovating houses than on building new ones. Building salvaging is now a $1 billion business.

• About 40% of construction waste is wood. Most recycled wood is turned into landscaping mulch or fuel.

• A recent study found that recycling and reusing building materials can keep 90% of construction debris out of garbage dumps.

• In some parts of the U.S., construction and demolition debris makes up as much as one-third of the solid waste in landfills.

SIMPLE THINGS YOU CAN DO

1. Find a Recycler

• A growing number of special processing facilities accept all building materials at one location. If you can't find one, look for a salvage yard that accepts lumber, plasterboard, bricks, metal, etc.

• Look in the Yellow Pages under "Salvage Materials," "Used Lumber," "Building Materials," "Scrap Dealers" and "Restoration."

• Some factories grind up scrap wood for use as a composting base or fuel. Call the public works department to see if there's one in your area. Note: not all wood is accepted—for instance, if it's painted with lead paint or varnish.

Juice cartons —known as "brick packs"— aren't recyclable.

• If you can't find a place to recycle: Have a garage sale. At the end of the day, put the unsold items on the curb with a "free" sign.

2. Recycle Building Materials
Windows & Doors
• Check wooden window frames. If they're rotten, they probably can't be salvaged. If they're sound and not crooked, they're reusable.
• Old solid wood doors are valuable; new ones are very expensive.
• If the bottom of a door is rotten, you may be able to salvage it by squaring it off. Otherwise, it may only be recyclable as scrap.
• Aluminum window frames are recyclable as scrap. You may be able to bring them in with your aluminum cans.

Lumber
• If you're planning to reuse 2 x 4's: Remove the nails immediately, even before transporting them. Use safety precautions when cutting; you never know when you'll run into a stray nail.

Sawdust
Use it with compost. It's like compost kitty litter—it absorbs moisture and odors. If you've got a lot, call a local landscaper or nursery.

Metal
• All metal (doorknobs, hinges, etc.) can be recycled (see p. 38). Copper or brass plumbing and electrical fixtures are prize salvage.
• Take used nails to a recycling center; don't bother trying to straighten and reuse them. Save screws, bolts and nuts.
• Old bathtubs and sinks are often made of cast iron coated with porcelain enamel. Salvage yards or scrap dealers may want them.

Bricks
• Used bricks are often collected by masonry firms and tumbled to take the edges off, so they look "aged." They may also be accepted with other building materials, to be ground up with concrete and used as a base for alleys and driveways.

FOR MORE INFORMATION
Renovation: A Complete Guide (2nd Edition). By Michael Litchfield (Prentice Hall, 1990). *The definitive single-volume book on restoring and renovating homes. Lots of info on reusing and recycling.*

Seattle-King County uses a roving "wastemobile" to pick up hazardous products.

THAT'S OIL, FOLKS

*Americans throw away enough used motor
oil every year to fill 120 supertankers.*

Have you ever seen used motor oil? Nothing could be dirtier; it's thick, black, and full of toxic engine crud.
Pretty disgusting, huh? It looks like it could never be cleaned...but it can. When motor oil is "re-refined," it's just as good as new. In fact, according to oil recyclers, motor oil never wears out; it can be re-refined and used forever.

WHY RECYCLE?

• Throwing oil in the trash—even in an airtight container—is just like pouring it on the ground. The oil will seep out and leach into groundwater when containers are crushed.

• A quart of motor oil can pollute 250,000 gallons of water.

• We make our own oil spills: About 62% of all oil-related pollution in the U.S. is caused by improper disposal of used motor oil.

• It costs only 10-20¢ a gallon to have used oil picked up for recycling, but $2-4 to drop it off at a hazardous waste collection site.

• Save resources: Evergreen Oil in Newark, California has developed a new process in which 62 gallons of new oil are recovered for every 100 gallons of old oil processed.

SIMPLE THINGS YOU CAN DO

Buy Recycled Oil

• Some oil which is re-refined is not necessarily labeled "recycled," because manufacturers fear that consumers won't buy it. Ask store managers which oils are re-refined, and buy them for everything—your lawnmower, snowmobile and car. Encourage others to buy it, too.

The Mobro garbage barge from Islip, NY, was turned away from 11 states and 5 countries.

If You Get Your Oil Changed At A Gas Station

• Check first to make sure they plan to recycle it. If not, take your car to a place that does.

If You Change Your Own Oil

1. Find a Place to Take It

• Many communities and states have oil recycling programs. The status is different in every state, and federal regulations are in flux. To find out what's going on in your community, check with your state recycling agency (see p. 117), or call your local fire department. If there's no program, tell local and state officials to set one up.

• Some gas stations, oil-changing outlets, and retailers take old oil and see that it gets recycled. It depends on where you live; in some states gas stations avoid it because of insurance issues. Call around.

• Last resort: Hazardous waste facilities take used motor oil. In fact, they often get more oil than anything else.

2. Recycle

• Don't mix solvents, water, or any other liquid waste in with it.

• Try to avoid getting it on the ground; it will leak into groundwater, or wash into rivers and streams.

• Store it in a container that won't leak and has a screw-on cap—a plastic gallon milk container, for example.

• There are several oil recycling kits on the market, generally available at hardware or automotive parts stores. They come with containers that double as oil-draining receptacles and carrying cases for transporting the oil to a recycling center.

Note: Do not confuse them with kits that make it easier to throw your oil away (they come with a kitty litter-type material that isn't recyclable; it all winds up in a landfill instead).

FOR MORE INFORMATION

• **"Recycling Used Oil."** EPA, Office of Solid Waste, 401 St. S.W., Washington, D.C. 20460. *Tells how to change and recycle your oil in 10 easy steps.*

• **Association of Petroleum Re-Refiners,** P.O. Box 427, Buffalo, NY 14205. *A trade organization of oil re-refiners. Write for information.*

Butcher paper and bakery paper can't be recycled.

GOODBYE, OL' PAINT

Americans buy 140 million gallons of latex paint each year —
enough to cover the entire state of Delaware with a coat of primer.

How much paint is stashed in your garage or basement? If you're an average American, you've got about about four gallons. And some day you'll have to decide what to do with it.

The easiest thing is to toss it in the garbage. But if you do that, you'll be polluting groundwater and soil; 300 toxic substances, including lead and mercury, have been found in commercial oil and latex paints. And since the EPA has designated paint a hazardous waste, you may also be breaking the law.

That leaves you with only two safe alternatives: Use your paint up (or give it to someone who will), or recycle it.

THE SEATTLE STORY

• In Seattle, Washington, large amounts of latex paint are being collected and mixed together in a test recycling program. Moldy or dirty paint is thrown out, along with all dark colors. Yellow and orange are also eliminated because they may contain lead. The rest is strained and blended.

• No matter what shades are mixed together, the paint always comes out beige. In recycling circles, the color is now called "Seattle Beige."

• About 45% of the latex paint collected in Seattle can be mixed and reused. This recycled paint is similar in quality to new paint, with a one year shelf life. Much of it goes to schools and hospitals.

SIMPLE THINGS YOU CAN DO

1. See what you've got

• To make recycling easier, first separate the oil-based paint from

As late as 1947, virtually 100% of all beverage bottles were returnable.

the latex paint, and the interior from the exterior paint.

• If you've had cans of paint sitting around for years, check to see if they're still usable. The paint could be dried out or moldy, even if the lids have been on the whole time. If the paint is unusable, you should dispose of what's left at a hazardous waste facility.

2. Find a Place to Recycle

• Some communities have paint exchange programs—"Drop & Swaps" where people bring resusable paint to trade or give away. Santa Monica, California, for example, has recirculated over 600 gallons of paint through its paint exchange program.

• Contact your local, county or state waste management officials to find out if there's a Drop & Swap in your area—or if they're willing to help start one.

• Since the EPA discovered mercury in some latex paints, there may be new guidelines for "Drop & Swaps." Check with city officials or your local waste management office to find out.

• Hazardous waste programs often collect and blend latex paint. Give your local facility a call.

3. Recycle

• *If your latex paints still look fresh:* Try mixing them together. The blend makes a good primer—or a final coat, if you like the color. Depending on the amount of paint and number of shades included, your primer may range in color from beige to grey to mud.

• *To recycle paint thinner:* Put used thinner in a jar. Let it settle for a while, then reuse the clean thinner on top, and let the sediment sink to the bottom. Eventually, you'll accumulate enough sediment to make disposal necessary. Again, a hazardous waste facility is the best alternative.

FOR MORE INFORMATION

• **Waste Watch Center,** 16 Haverhill St., Andover, MA 01810. *Send $1 and a self-addressed, stamped envelope for info on new latex paint guidelines.*

• **"Paint Disposal...The Right Way."** National Paint and Coating Association, 1500 Rhode Island Ave N.W., Washington, D.C. 20005. *A free brochure.*

Alabama recycled 6 million gallons of motor oil in 1988.

WHAT A LOAD OF SCRAP

If you stacked all the refrigerators Americans buy in a single week, you'd have a tower more than 80 miles high.

W hat happens to old refrigerators and stoves? It might not seem important, since many of us only deal with the question a few times in our lives. But multiply it by millions of families, and you've got a serious disposal problem.

Used appliances don't have to wind up in a dump, or on the side of the road. With a small effort—like a simple phone call to a non-profit organization or scrap dealer—you can insure that your old appliance is repaired and reused, or that the materials are recycled.

PCB TROUBLE

• Appliances have traditionally been collected by scrap dealers, who shred the metal and sell it to steel mills to be recycled.

• But in the mid-1970s, it was determined that motors in some appliances were hazardous because they contained highly toxic *polychlorinated biphenyls*—PCBs. In 1979, the EPA banned PCBs.

• PCBs pollute the air when appliances are shredded, and can contaminate soil or groundwater when landfilled. Their presence turned standard appliance recycling into an environmental hazard.

• Now scrap dealers, afraid of inadvertantly turning their business locations into toxic waste sites, are cautious about accepting appliances. Special care is taken to remove motors before shredding.

• It's worth the trouble, though. If all the appliances Americans throw away were recycled instead, we would keep 500,000 to 600,000 pounds of toxic PCBs out of landfills every year.

SIMPLE THINGS TO DO

1. Check for Environmental Hazards

• Refrigerators, freezers and air conditioners contain ozone-

The city of Philadelphia ships its waste as far away as Ohio.

depleting CFCs as a coolant. When they need to be scrapped, the CFCs should be taken out and recycled (see p. 98).

(see p. 98)

• For safety's sake, take off refrigerator doors; every year kids get trapped in discarded refrigerators and suffocate.

• Does the appliance have a motor that could contain PCBs? If it was made before 1980, it might. Call the manufacturer to find out.

• If it does have PCBs, you should remove the "drive motor capacitor" and deliver it to a hazardous waste facility. Then it can go to a scrap yard. If you need more information, call a scrap metal dealer for advice.

• Air conditioners are the appliances most likely to contain PCBs. Most water heaters, washers and dryers don't have them. Since stoves don't usually contain either motors or refrigerants, they should be easy to recycle.

2. Donate Old Appliances

• Nonprofits like Goodwill Industries, St.Vincent DePaul Society, and the Salvation Army will generally accept old appliances if they work.

• In many parts of the country (where space is available), they hold daily "as is" auctions to sell off items that need repair.

• This is one of the most effective ways to recycle appliances. The appliances are bought and repaired by flea marketeers, or smaller thrift shop operators, who then resell them to the public.

• Different organizations have different collection policies. Check around.

3. Recycle for Scrap

• Consult your local recycling center or scrap metal dealers. Look in the Yellow Pages under "Scrap Metal" and "Recycling."

• Scrap metal dealers should be able to tell you how to prepare your appliance so they can accept it.

• If they don't pick up appliances, they may be able to connect you with individuals or companies who do.

• Last resort: The retailer who sells you a new appliance might be willing to haul the old one away (although it may cost you a few bucks). Make sure they plan to recycle.

The compacting garbage truck, called the "Packer," was introduced in 1950.

ALL TIRED OUT

*Americans throw out more than 250 million tires
every year—about one tire for every person.*

What are we going to do with all the tires we throw away?
So far, there's no single, established way to recycle
them. But businesses are getting creative about it. They're
turning tires into roads, brake linings, reefs…and new tires. There
may be recycling in your area soon—next time you buy a new tire,
check around.

TIRE RECYCLING NEWS

• One of the most promising ways to recycle is by turning them
into ground rubber "crumbs" and add them to asphalt for paving
roads, running tracks, runways, playgrounds. The result: pavement
life is increased four to five times.

• In 1989, 24 million pounds of rubber (about 2.5 million tires)
were converted to "asphalt-rubber." It's been used in 35 states.

• Recycled rubber can also be used in boat bumpers, carpet pad-
ding, and wire and pipe insulation.

• People in Third World countries know the value of used tires. In
India, they cut up tire scraps to make inexpensive shoes.

• Retreading is still the most common form of tire recycling.
Currently, about one-fifth of the vehicle tires made in the U.S. are
retreaded. If your tire casing is in good shape, it may be recycled as
a retread.

HOW ARE TIRES RECYCLED?

• Tires are made of petroleum, steel belts and synthetic fibers (only
about 10% of the average tire is real latex).

• They're shredded into two-inch rubber squares, flattened with
rollers, and then ground into even smaller, half-inch bits.

• Steel wires and threads (about 60% of the tire) are then
removed. The rubber pieces are cleaned and bagged and sold to
various manufacturers.

All major towns in Oregon have curbside collection for motor oil.

WHY RECYCLE?

• About eight out of every ten tires in America wind up in landfills or on tire "stockpiles."

• Tires collect gases released by decomposing garbage, then float up through the trash and pop out.

• This problem has prompted landfill operators to turn away tires, so many end up on big "tire piles." When they catch fire (which happens fairly often), these piles release toxic chemicals that cause acid rain—and the fires can burn for months.

• Each burning tire can leach 2 -1/2 gallons of waste oil into the ground, threatening groundwater.

• Making a pound of rubber out of recycled materials saves about 75% of the energy needed to produce one pound of virgin rubber.

SIMPLE THINGS YOU CAN DO

1. Precycle

• The best way to cut tire waste is to buy long life tires and extend their wear by taking care of them.

• Keep them properly inflated; you'll increase your gas mileage by up to 5%. Check the air pressure every two weeks.

• Rotate and balance tires every 6,000 miles; keep wheels aligned.

2. Pick the Right Dealer

If tire recycling (rubber asphalt, etc.) is available in your area, patronize dealers who guarantee they'll recycle your old tires. At the moment, there's not a whole lot more you can do.

FOR MORE INFORMATION

• **Directory of Scrap Tire Processors by State,** Rubber Manufacturers Association, 1400 K St. NW, Washington, D.C. 20005; (202) 682-4800. *A free listing of firms that recycle tires.*

• **"Glove Compartment Tire Safety and Mileage Kit."** Available from the Tire Industry Safety Council, P.O. Box 1801, Washington, D.C., 20013. *Cost: $4. Includes an air pressure gauge, a tread depth gauge, four tire valve caps, and a 12-page "consumer tire guide."*

Japan recycles more than half its household and commercial waste.

HOLD ON TO CFCs

According to the Natural Resources Defense Council,
car air conditioners are responsible
for 16% of the depletion of the ozone layer.

You've heard about the ozone hole. Here's something you can do to help keep it from getting bigger: Keep CFCs—the coolants in your refrigerator or air conditioner—out of the atmosphere by recycling them.

CLEARING THE AIR

• When CFCs are released they float into the upper atmosphere, where they act like little Pac-Men, eating away the ozone that protects us from the sun's ultraviolet rays.

• When the ozone layer is damaged, skin cancer increases and wildlife suffers. There is even speculation that plankton, the essential rung at the bottom of the food chain, might die out, which could be lethal to all life.

• The CFCs that are released today will take 8-12 years to get to the ozone layer and can reman there for dozens of years. So even if we stop all leaks now, we're faced with decades of ozone depletion.

SIMPLE THINGS YOU CAN DO

• New machines, nicknamed *vampires* because they "suck" coolants out of appliances and trap them in bottles for recycling, are increasingly common at service stations and repair shops.

• When you get your car air conditioner serviced, pick a mechanic who uses a "vampire," rather than letting it evaporate.

• Be sure your home air conditioner and refrigerator are serviced by a CFCs recycler, too.

FOR MORE INFORMATION

An NRDC Earth Action Guide: Saving the Ozone Layer."
Natural Resources Defense Council, 40 W. 20th St., New York, NY 10011. *A pamphlet available for $1.*

Every day, Americans recycle about 13 million glass bottles and jars.

THE CARTRIDGE FAMILY

Cartridge recycling is a $90 million a year business.

When your laser printer starts spitting out faded-looking copies, you're probably more concerned about putting a new cartridge in than you are about dealing with the old one. Chances are, you just toss the old one into the garbage; after all, it's "disposable."

But there's an alternative: Have that foot-long plastic cartridge cleaned and refilled, and it can be used three to six more times. What's more, recyclers will make it easy for you; they often pick up cartridges for free, or pay for shipping them back and forth.

WHY RECYCLE?

• It's estimated that over 16 million laser printer cartridges are used every year. About 14 million of them go into landfills.

• It gets worse: By 1993, we'll be using an estimated 34 million cartridges every year. Unless we start recycling more, we'll be throwing away more than 28 million a year.

• It costs about 40% less (about $50) to refill a cartridge than it does to buy a new one.

SIMPLE THINGS YOU CAN DO

• Ask your local computer dealer if a reputable company in your area recycles laser printer cartridges—over 4,000 firms already do.

• If you can't find one, contact the American Cartridge Recycling Association (ACRA), 1717 Bayshore Dr., Suite 2434, Miami, FL 33132; (305) 539-0701. They'll refer you to one of their members.

• You can also donate your old cartridges to ACRA; proceeds will help educate recycling entrepreneurs.

Germany recycles almost 40% of its glass.

ODDS & ENDS

One person's trash is another's treasure.

This is the page we saved for leftovers—things that didn't fit, or didn't really need their own pages...but in the great recycling tradition, we didn't want to let them go to waste.

• **Books:** Like phone books, both paperbacks and hardbacks have glue in the bindings; so they're not easily recyclable. Try selling them to used book stores, or donate them to libraries, schools, etc.

• **Furniture:** Goodwill or The Salvation Army say they'll take chairs, mattresses, etc. in good condition. They'll pick up from your house; but, you may have to haul the items downstairs if you live upstairs.

• If it's a ripped or broken piece of furniture, look in the Yellow Pages under "Charity Organizations." Someone may accept and repair it.

• **TVs and Stereos:** Give or sell them to a friend, or advertise them in the newspaper. If you donate them to non-profit organizations (i.e. youth or church groups); it's a tax write off.

THE UNRECYCLABLES:

• **Butcher & Baker Paper:** They have a plastic lining.
• **Overnight Envelopes:** they're made with plastic fibers.
• **Disposable Diapers:** They're paper with plastic liners. The diaper industry is promoting them as compostable or recyclable, but they really aren't at this time.
• **Household Batteries:** These aren't being recycled right now, but don't throw them away! They contain heavy metals and belong at a household hazardous waste facility.
• **Juice Boxes:** Also known as "Brick Packs," can't be recycled, they're made of aluminum foil, paper *and* plastic.
• **Paper Milk Cartons:** Although they're paperboard, they've got a plastic coating inside.
• **Photographs:** They're coated with chemicals.
• **Plastic Containers:** Any that are classified #7 on the bottom are made with unrecyclable plastic.
• **Tea Bags:** The tea is a problem; but you can compost them.

Newsprint is the easiest kind of paper to recycle, because it has no chemicals or fillers.

GETTING
MORE

INVOLVED

STARTING AN OFFICE RECYCLING PROGRAM

Most of us spend a big part of the day at work. So, to make recycling a real part of your life, you'll want to recycle at the office, too. To help, we've answered some often-asked questions on the subject. But this is by no means a definitive work on office recycling. If you're serious about getting a program started, send away for the materials listed at the end of this section. They're comprehensive...and inspiring.

IS OUR OFFICE TOO BIG FOR RECYCLING?
• No office is ever too large for a recycling program. In fact, the bigger a business is, the more lucrative the recycling operation is.
• If your company is a law firm, insurance company, bank or government office you probably have paper coming out of your ears.
• Find out how much paper your office generates. The rule of thumb is .5 pounds per day for each employee. That's 2.5 pounds a week; 130 pounds a year—per person!

WELL THEN, IS OUR OFFICE TOO SMALL?
• An office is never too small to recycle either, but you may run into a snag getting someone to pick it up. Talk to businesses in your building (or nearby) and see if they want to recycle, too. By joining together, you'll generate more material and make it worthwhile for a collector to pick up from you.
• Check with your local government office to see if they can help.
• If you still can't get a collector, you can always drop off the materials yourself at a recycling center.

WHO'LL TAKE IT?
The first thing to do is find someone to take your office paper. Ask the local recycling center for referrals—they may have a list of companies already picking up from businesses in your area. Otherwise, look in the Yellow Pages under "Waste Paper" or "Recycling."

The cars recycled in 1988 would fill a parking lot 4 miles long by 5 miles wide.

WHAT DO WE ASK THE HAULER WHEN WE CALL?
• What materials will they take?
• How much will they pay you for each material (white paper, computer paper, newspaper, etc.)?
• Will they sign a long-term (i.e. one year) contract?
• How often will they make pick-ups?
• Note: Does your company destroy confidential documents? That's important to know because recyclers usually can't accept shredded paper; it doesn't mix well with the rest of the paper.

WHERE DO WE PUT RECYCLABLES?
• Everybody should have a desktop container, with separate compartments for different kinds of paper. When it's full, each person dumps it into a larger bin (e.g. in the coffee room). Put up colorful signs near the recycling bins. Also, clearly mark the bins so people won't mistake them for trash cans.
• Most programs work best when they're integrated with the trash disposal system. In a lot of offices, the maintenance people simply transfer the materials in the central bins to a storage area in the basement or at the loading dock.

WHO TAKES RESPONSIBILITY FOR THE PROGRAM?
• It's a good idea to have a recycling committee. Select one individual to act as a liaison among employees, management, janitorial staff and the collectors who pick up your materials.
• Every division or floor (say, every 30 employees) should have a recycling coordinator. These people can answer questions and check to make sure people aren't putting trash in the recycling bins.

HOW DO WE SPREAD THE WORD?
• Your recycling program will work best if management supports it, and if everyone knows about it ahead of time. Have the CEO write a memo about the program, discussing the benefits, where the revenue will go, etc.
•Publicize the program in the corporate newsletter and send out flyers.

The U.S. exports more waste paper than any other country.

WHAT CAN WE RECYCLE BESIDES PAPER?
• Office paper is the main attraction at businesses, but you should be able to find someone to pick up bottles, cans, newspapers or other materials if you have enough of them. Ask your paper collector if any other materials are accepted; if not, ask for a referral to a company that may take them..
• Look through the "Material World" section of this book to see if your company can recycle anything else.

WHAT MORE CAN WE DO?
• Encourage the people in charge of buying supplies to buy recycled paper. It's a powerful way to "vote" for recycling by helping increase the demand for recycled products. In many cases, recycled office and computer papers cost about the same as non-recycled paper.
• Start an office policy of recycling laser printer toner cartridges (see P. 99 for details).
• Precycle: If your firm uses a lot of packing material (like foam "peanuts") find a way to decrease it. Why not use your shredded paper as packing material?
• Bring a mug from home to discourage the use of disposable cups.

CAN WE MAKE MONEY BY RECYCLING?
• Many businesses are making money by saving on disposal costs and selling recyclables.
• A case in point: The Hyatt Regency Chicago set up a recycling center this year. They expect to save $100,000 in waste hauling charges and take in $200,000 by selling materials that were once considered garbage.

FOR MORE INFORMATION
• Contact your local or state recycling office—they'll probably have a brochure that can give you the details on starting office recycling.
• **"Your Office Paper Recycling Guide,"** San Francisco Recycling Program, Room 271 City Hall, San Francisco, CA 94102. *A wonderful booklet; $5. Make checks out to City and County of San Francisco.*
• **"Office Paper Recycling."** Earth Care Paper Co. PO Box 3335 Madison, WI 53704; (608) 256-5522. *Cost: $2.50, Catalog #8319.*

Paper products use about 35% of the world's annual commercial wood harvest.

STARTING A SCHOOL RECYCLING PROGRAM

Is your school teaching the three 'Rs'? We're not talking about *Reading, Writing and 'Rithmetic*—teachers have that part handled. We mean *Reduce, Reuse, Recycle.* How about starting a recycling program at your school? Here's a pop quiz (with answers supplied) to get you started.

DOES IT REALLY WORK?

Absolutely. Some states and communities have laws requiring schools to recycle. But there are also successful voluntary school recycling programs all over the country. One example: the Midlothian Middle School near Richmond, Virginia collected 125,000 aluminum cans in two days. They earned more than $2,000 for the science department.

IS MONEY THE MAIN BENEFIT?

That depends on your goals. At the Midlothian school, the fact that the program could earn money was an important factor in getting the school administration's support.

• But there are other considerations: There's a growing understanding that children must learn good ecological habits at school. If we don't help kids develop a respect for the Earth when they're young, they'll be fighting an uphill battle when they get older—as most grown-ups are now.

• Oh, yes—and let's not forget the resources we'll save when every school in America recycles.

HOW DO YOU KNOW THAT A SCHOOL PROGRAM HELPS KIDS APPRECIATE RECYCLING?

Common sense, for one thing. But if that's not enough, years ago Reynolds Aluminum did a study. The results: "The actual practice of recycling changes attitudes. This is an important point—merely studying about recycling may not change people's attitudes to a favorable view of recycling, but the practice of recycling does."

Which country has the highest aluminum recycling rate? The Netherlands.

OKAY, HOW DO WE GET STARTED?
Form a committee of people who are interested in recycling at the school. It doesn't have to be a crowd, but you should include some administrators, teachers, students, and if possible, at least one janitor. Choose one person to be the representative for the group. Finding people who are interested in recycling should be fairly easy these days—how about bringing it up at a PTA or Student Council meeting?

NEXT STEP?
Decide what you have that can be recycled. The easiest way is to empty a garbage can onto a tarp, and check out what's in it. Make a list of the recyclable things. Ask the janitor for observations, too.

• If you want to take this a step further, conduct an informal analysis of the trash. Take a representative sample of trash and separate it into different materials to figure out the proportions. Figure out how much the school spends on trash bills, then determine how much less it would cost if some of the more prevalent items were eliminated. Think about what kind of storage space you'll have for these recyclables. If it's not much space, consider just recycling aluminum cans and white paper (which are the most profitable).

WHAT MATERIALS AM I LIKELY TO FIND?
• Some of the more common school recyclables: white paper, other paper (e.g., construction), cans, bottles, newspapers, boxes.

WHO'LL PICK IT UP?
• Do a little research to find out. There might be a city-run program...or you can have a private hauler do it. Check with your local government office first, then look in the phone book under "Recycling" and call up some of the companies listed there.

WHO'S IN CHARGE?
• Select a few coordinators—students, teachers, administrators or even parents. One can act as go-between for the school and the hauler. Another can work with school administrators. Others can organize recycling in each classroom, the cafeteria, etc.

The first incinerator was commissioned in New York City in 1885.

HOW WILL IT WORK IN EACH CLASS?

In each classroom a student is designated "recycling monitor." (They can rotate every week.) Monitors should make sure that recyclables do not end up in the trash and that contaminants (i.e. glue) don't wind up in the recycling bins.

• Decide who'll collect the materials from the classroom recycling bins and take them to the storage area.

WHERE DO WE PUT RECYCLABLES?

Put recycling bins next to trash cans. Put paper bins in offices and classrooms, and bins for bottles and cans in the cafeteria, or wherever people eat. Mark each bin clearly. It's amazing how people mistake recycling bins for trash cans!

• Note: Your school's fire code may require that bins for storing paper be fireproof (metal or fire resistant plastic with a lid) if they're in the halls. Check it out.

WHAT MORE CAN WE DO?

Ask yourselves "What's left in the trash that isn't being recycled? Are there ways to reduce that trash at the source?" For example, are teachers having students use both sides of the paper?

• Buy recycled products. If you really want to support recycling in your community, think about having the school buy recycled items like office paper, tissues and toilet paper. And students can use recycled notebook paper.

FOR MORE INFORMATION

• **The Information Center** (05-305), US EPA, 401 M Street SW, Washington, D.C. 20460. *Send for a listing of curriculum, how- to guides for recycling, and other classroom materials.*

• **Reynolds Aluminum Recycling Company.** *Call (800)228-2525 for info on aluminum recycling programs in a school setting.*

Most paper mills own their own forests.

RECYCLING IN AN APARTMENT BUILDING

L ive in an apartment building? Are you and your neighbors suffering from "curbside envy?" Well here's the cure: Start your own recycling program.

CAN APARTMENTS HAVE CURBSIDE RECYCLING?
Not the same type as houses. Generally, apartment buildings have limited space for storing recyclables, and with so many people involved, a lot of organizing is needed. Plus, apartment curbside recycling can be a problem for collectors, because they have to empty large dumpsters instead of small bins.

CAN OUR APARTMENT HAVE SOME OTHER KIND OF RECYCLING PROGRAM, THEN?
Yes, if you can coordinate it with all the residents in the building, and find someone to pick up the materials.

HOW MANY TENANTS HAVE TO PARTICIPATE?
The more people participating, the more materials you generate, and that's important. If there aren't enough materials, it won't be cost effective, and then you won't be able to attract a collector.

WHAT CAN WE RECYCLE?
It varies, according to your collector, but it's usually a combination of newspaper, bottles, cans, and other kinds of paper.

HOW DO WE APPROACH THE BUILDING MANAGER?
Mention that recycling can really save money because there will be less trash the building has to pay to have hauled away. Let him or her know that it might *make* money if enough materials are recycled.

HOW DO WE FIND SOMEONE TO PICK IT UP?
If you know someone in another building that's already recycling, ask what company they're using. Otherwise, ask for suggestions from your trash collector, try your local recyling office, or look in the Yellow Pages under "Recycling."

Recycling half the world's paper would free 20 million acres of forestland.

WHERE DO WE PUT ALL THE STUFF?

Even though your building may not have tons of space to store recyclables, scout around and see what space might be used. And remember, if you start recycling, you'll have less trash, so maybe you can use some of that extra space for recycling bins.

• Besides your standard garbage and trash area, look in the utility and laundry rooms. There may be room there for smaller bins.

• Then, determine how much recyclable material you'll have each week. The rule of thumb is about 3.5 pounds of materials per unit in the building. But when you start your program, someone should check to see how much you really have as people get the hang of recycling.

WHO'LL BE RESPONSIBLE FOR THE PROGRAM?

It'll be easiest if you and your neighbors can share the responsibility. Get at least one coordinator per floor, or one person for about every 50 residents. Bins should be checked every now and then to make sure they're being used correctly.

• If maintenance people will be overseeing the recycling, you may not even need coordinators. It all depends on your building.

HOW DO WE GET EVERYONE TO RECYCLE?

The more convenient it is for people to recycle, the more likely they'll be to do it. For example, if the building has 5 stories, it's best to put small bins on each floor where residents can put their materials—so people don't have to trek down to the garage all the time.

• Before the program starts, send around a memo with recycling guidelines so everyone knows what to expect, and what to do.

• After the program has been running for a while, let the residents know how it's going. Send out a newsletter that tells how much money and resources have been saved so far, any problems they should know about, etc.

• Have a party for all the building residents using any money earned from your joint recycling efforts.

FOR MORE INFORMATION

Strength In Numbers: Recycling in Multi-Family Housing *is a 10-minute VHS video that you can borrow by sending a $16 deposit to:* Association of New Jersey Environmental Commissions, 300 Mendham Road, Route 24, Box 157, Mendham, New Jersey 07945.

States with bottle deposit laws have 35-40% less litter by volume.

HOW TO START A RECYCLING CENTER

Over 3000 recycling centers were started after the first Earth Day in 1970—but few of them really took off. The public became indifferent and cities were reluctant to invest in additional equipment for sorting.

Today, it's a different story. People are starting to understand the need to do something positive to help solve the garbage and resource crisis. We're ready to recycle, but often find there's no place in the community to take our bottles, cans, etc. If your town isn't recycling, this should help you get started.

IS IT REALLY POSSIBLE?
You bet, and no town is too small.
• A case in point is Elloree, South Carolina, population 903. Volunteers of "Recycle Elloree" collect materials within a 20 mile radius. They've got so much support that the last town meeting voted to start curbside recycling. This will save the community $30,000 annually (almost half their annual garbage cost).
•Wellesley, Massachusetts has the ultimate drop-off recycling center at the town dump. It has picnic tables, manicured lawns—people go there to spend the afternoon. Do the picnickers recycle? About 90% of them do—contributing mainly newspaper, glass, cardboard and aluminum.

SO HOW DO WE GET STARTED ?
• First, check to see if any nearby towns are recycling. If so, find out if the collectors are able to expand into your area.
• See if your state has a recycling association (look in the appendix to check it out). They can offer you helpful advice (i.e. finding large bins, haulers, etc.).
• Contact successful recycling programs to see how they got started (look in the appendix for books with case studies).
• Form a committee. Have each member do something to get it going.

Half of the paper America consumes is used to wrap and decorate consumer products.

WHO WILL BUY THE STUFF WE COLLECT?

Make sure there's a market for the materials. Look in the Yellow
Pages under "Recyclers" and "Resource Recovery." If there are no
local listings, look under the same headings in a state-wide business
to business directory or another regional directory.

WHAT SHOULD WE ASK THE COMPANY TAKING OUR RECYCLABLES?

• What materials will they take? How much will they pay for each
material (by the ton)?

• Will they provide the bins or do you need to have your own
containers?

• Will they pick up the materials or do they need to be taken somewhere?

• How should the materials be prepared (e.g. should newspapers be
bundled or dumped out loose)?

WHERE DO WE PUT THE CENTER?

You'll need to find a place to collect and store the materials.

• An important factor: a convenient location. Ask a centrally-
located civic organization, church, school, or store if you can set up
in their parking lot. Or find a vacant lot on public property and ask
city hall if you can use it temporarily.

• Landfills and transfer stations may be good places to try, if people
go there often (i.e., if your community has no trash collection
service).

Note: It helps if the space is easily accessible to cars and trucks.

WHO IS GOING TO RUN THE COLLECTION CENTER?

If your government isn't ready to help you recycle, your best bet is to
try setting up recycling on a voluntary basis. Once your government
officials see that people *want* to recycle—and they will—they'll be
more likely to get involved.

• Have volunteers. When you first start, open the center part time.
Weekends are the best time for most people to drop stuff off.

HOW DO WE RUN A RECYCLING CENTER?

Volunteers or staff check the bins to make sure the right materials

Packaging makes up a third of our trash.

are in the right bins. Ideally, one person should do this consistently; he or she can also prevent people from dumping non-recyclables. (If materials slip by with contaminants in them, you might have to pay for them to be sorted later.)
• Post easy-to-read instructions for people to follow. Make sure the bins are clearly marked. This will make the job easier.

HOW DO WE LET EVERYONE KNOW ABOUT IT?
Give yourselves some time to publicize the center. Educating people is a key factor in the success of your drop-off site.
• Recycling is news in the '90's; so ask local newspapers and radio stations to mention the campaign. Have flyers printed listing days and hours the center will be open—post and distribute them.
• Make sure you mention the sponsoring organization (if you have one) in your publicity materials. And ask them to mention the recycling program if they send out a newsletter.

WHAT'S NEXT?
A full-scale government recycling program should be your next goal.
• Once you've established a popular drop-off center in your community, get the people who recycle there on a regular basis together. Petition your city officials to sponsor the center, or fund a more convenient curbside program.
• You can also consider opening a buyback center. It will attract people who prefer making money by recycling, but it's more of a financial risk.

FOR MORE INFORMATION
• **"Ten Steps to Organizing a Community Recycling Program."** Pennsylvania Resources Council, P.O. Box 88, Media, PA 19063.
• **"Recycling: A Local Solution to the Solid Waste Crisis."** Local Government Commission Inc., 909 12th Street, Suite 205, Sacramento, CA 95814. *A series of guides; $8.50 each, $37.50 together.*
• **The National Recycling Coalition,** 1101 30th Street, NW, Washington DC 20007; (202)625-6406. *Ask for information for communities interested in recycling. Include a self-addressed, stamped envelope.*
• **Environmental Defense Fund,** 257 Park Ave. South, NY, NY 10010, (212) 505-2100. *Write for the free brochure and publications list.*

A "reverse-vending machine" in Dickenson, SD, reclaimed 109 tons of cans in a year.

BUYING RECYCLED PRODUCTS

So you're recycling? Well, that's a good start. But there's more to it than just returning your cans; are you buying recycled products, too?

WHY IS IT IMPORTANT TO BUY RECYCLED PRODUCTS?

As WorldWatch says, "there is no cycle in recycle until a throwaway is reused." In other words, if we don't buy recycled products, there won't be a market for them.

• Manufacturers have always assumed that consumers prefer things made with new material. We know they're wrong, but we've got to show them. When they can make money by using recycled materials, they'll support recycling.

WHAT CAN I BUY THAT'S RECYCLED?

Plenty. For starters, paper items like tissue, paper towels, cereal boxes, napkins, bags, writing paper, greeting cards, and padded envelopes.

• You might be surprised to find motor oil, retreaded tires, and plastic bins on the list. And don't forget the staples: bottles and cans.

• For a comprehensive list of brand-name recycled products, send $3.50 to the Pennsylvania Resources Council, 25 West 3rd St., Media, PA 19063; (215) 565-9131.

HOW DO I KNOW WHAT'S RECYCLED?

• First, look for the recycling symbol with the three arrows rotating clockwise. It tells you that the product is either made with recycled content...or that it's potentially recyclable.

• For example, paper companies use the three arrows on a dark background to indicate "made from recycled paper." Three arrows with *no* background means "recyclable." How to tell if cereal, cracker and cake mix boxes are recycled: they're gray inside.

• Don't be sidetracked by the term "recyclable", it just means the product *can be* recycled. In fact, according to *The Green Consumer*, you can assume that if a package is simply called "recyclable," it contains *no* recycled content.

Every year, Americans harvest as much grass from lawns as the Japanese harvest rice.

IF IT SAYS "RECYCLED," HOW CAN I BE SURE IT IS?
• You can't always. Some products are made from scraps off the cutting room floor—but the companies call it recycled paper. Look for the word "post-consumer" on recycled products—that means it's made from paper that people have already used.

WHERE CAN I BUY RECYCLED PRODUCTS?
• Try the same places you buy regular products. You may not find them yet, because the demand for non-recycled products is still higher than the demand for recycled ones. But keep asking: retailers will get the message.

I'VE TRIED TO FIND RECYCLED PRODUCTS, BUT CAN'T. WHAT CAN I DO?
• Let store managers and product manufacturers know you want them. Suggest the store carry them, or start its own line of recycled products. If enough people speak up, they'll change their ways.

While you're at it, encourage the government to recycle—local, state and federal government purchases make up about 20% of the Gross National Product—if they got involved, it would really boost the market for recycled products.

ARE RECYCLED PRODUCTS MORE EXPENSIVE?
• Right now, most products are still made with virgin material, because recycling is just catching on. Demand for non-recycled products is still higher than the demand for recycled ones. As a result, you might have to pay a little more for them now, but experts expect prices to drop as more people buy recycled and demand increase.

DOES ALL RECYCLED PAPER LOOK LIKE IT'S BEEN RECYCLED?
• Definitely not. While some types of recycled paper are brown or gray because they're unbleached, there are many types that look just as good as virgin stock. In fact, the paper you're looking at right now is 80% post-consumer recycled paper.

Compost helpers: There are an average of 2.7 million worms in every acre of land.

GETTING A JOB
IN RECYCLING

So you think you deal with a lot of garbage at work now? Well, some people handle tons of garbage every day at work...and love it. That's because they're working in waste management or recycling—not only helping save the environment, but often making good money doing it. Here's how to get started.

DO I NEED SPECIAL TRAINING?
If you want a technical job, you'll probably need a degree in environmental studies. But many other jobs are available in areas like public relations, office management, etc. And because it's a new industry and there aren't many highly-qualified candidates, what you know may not be as important as enthusiasm and willingness to learn.
• Another way to get in the door: hands-on experience. Even a little volunteering for your community drop-off center will help convince employers that you know something about their business.

HOW DO I FIND THAT KIND OF JOB?
• Get the inside track: Go to industry conferences and meet people; you might hear about positions by word-of-mouth. It's much better than being one of the many job-seekers applying for environment-related jobs advertised in the paper.
• Contact your local, county or state government—many of these offices are hiring recycling coordinators.
• Do some research on private companies in the waste management business. Find out what kinds of jobs they offer, what skills you'd need, etc. Then approach them and explain how your skills could match their needs.
• For the entrepreneur: The recycling field is ideal because many communities don't have recycling yet. You can get it started.

FOR MORE INFORMATION
• **The CEIP Fund**, 68 Harrison Ave., Boston, MA 02111; (617) 426-4375. *Publishes* The Complete Guide to Environmental Careers, *with a section on solid waste management.*
• *Check the classified job listings in* **Resource Recycling** *and* **Biocycle** *Magazines (see P. 127).*

When tin cans were invented, only 5 or 6 could be made per hour.

RESOURCES

STATE RECYCLING AGENCIES

If you want information about recycling in your state—from a list of buyback centers to updates on pending recycling legislation, call your state recycling agency. They also have excellent brochures and school curriculum information on recycling.

EPA • *Office of Solid Waste*, 401 M St. S.W., Washington, D.C. 20460, (202) 382-4610. Hotline: (800) 424-9346.

ALABAMA • *Department of Environmental Management*, Solid Waste Branch, Land Division, 1751 Congressman Dickinson Dr., Montgomery, AL 36130, (205) 271-7700.

ALASKA • *Department of Environmental Conservation*, Recycling, P.O. Box O, Juneau, AK 99811-1800, (907) 465-2671.

ARIZONA • *Department of Environmental Quality*, Waste Planning Section, 4th Floor, 2005 N. Central Ave., Phoenix, AZ 85004, (602) 257-2372.
Department of Commerce, Energy Office, 3800 N. Central, Suite 1200, Phoenix, AZ 85012, (800) 352-5499.

ARKANSAS • *Pollution Control & Ecology*, Solid Waste Management Division, 8001 National Dr., Little Rock, AR 72219, (501) 562-7444.

CALIFORNIA • *Department of Conservation*, Division of Recycling, 1025 P St., Sacramento, CA 95814, (916) 323-3743. For your nearest recycling center call (800) 332-SAVE. For general information on beverage container recycling call (800) 642-5669.
Integrated Waste Management, 1020 Ninth St., Suite 300, Sacramento, CA 95814, (916) 322-3330.

COLORADO • *Department of Health*, Hazardous Materials & Waste Management Division, 4210 E. 11th Ave., Room 351, Denver, CO 80220, (303) 331-4830.

Plastic bottles can be recycled to make paint brush bristles.

CONNECTICUT • *Department of Recycling*, State Office Bldg., 165 Capitol Ave., Hartford, CT 06106, (203) 566-8722.

DELAWARE • *Department of Natural Resources & Environmental Control*, Division of Air & Waste Management, P.O. Box 1401, 89 Kings Highway, Dover, DE 19903, (302) 739-3820.

DISTRICT OF COLUMBIA • *Office of Recycling*, 65 K St., Lower Level, Washington, D.C. 20002, (202) 939-7116.

FLORIDA • *Department of Environmental Regulation*, Division of Waste Management, 2600 Blairstone Rd., Tallahassee, FL 32399-2400, (904) 488-0300.

GEORGIA • *Department of Natural Resources*, Environmental Protection Division, 3420 Norman Berry Dr., 7th Floor, Hapeville, GA 30354, (404) 656-2836.
Department of Community Affairs, 1200 Equitable Bldg., 100 Peachtree St., Atlanta, GA 30303, (404) 656-3898.

HAWAII • *Department of Health*, Solid & Hazardous Waste Division, 5 Waterfront Plaza, Suite 250, 500 Ala-Moana Blvd., Honolulu, HI 96813, (808) 543-8227.

IDAHO • *Division of Environmental Quality*, IWRAP Bureau, Hazardous Materials Branch, 1410 N. Hilton, Boise, ID 83706, (208) 334-5879.

ILLINOIS • *Office of Solid Waste & Renewable Resources*, 325 W. Adams, Springfield, IL 62704-1892, (217) 524-5454.

INDIANA • *Department of Environmental Management*, Office of Pollution Prevention and Technical Assistance, 105 S. Meridian St., Indianapolis, IN 46225, (317) 232-8172. (800) 451-6027.

IOWA • *Department of Natural Resources*, Waste Management Authority Division, 900 E. Grand Ave., Des Moines, IA 50319, (515) 281-8176.

KANSAS • *Department of Health & Environment*, Department of Solid Waste Management, Building 740, Forbes Field, Topeka, KS 66620, (913) 296-1590.

Paper makes up about 41% of our trash.

KENTUCKY • *Division of Waste Management*, Resources Recovery Branch, 18 Reilly Rd., Frankfort, KY 40601, (502) 564-6716.

LOUISIANA • *Department of Environmental Quality*, P.O. Box 44066, Baton Rouge, LA 70804-4096, (504) 342-9103.

MAINE • *Waste Management Agency*, State House Station #154, Augusta, ME 04333, (207) 289-5300.

MARYLAND • *Department of Environmental Quality*, Hazardous Waste Program, 2500 Broening Highway, Building 40, 2nd Floor, Baltimore, MD 21224, (301) 631-3343.

MASSACHUSETTS • *Department of Environmental Protection*, Division of Solid Waste Management, 1 Winter St., 4th Floor, Boston, MA 02108, (617) 292-5980.

MICHIGAN • *Dept. of Natural Resources*, Waste Management Division, P.O. Box 30241, Lansing, MI 48909, (517) 373-2730.

MINNESOTA • *Office of Waste Management*, 1350 Energy Lane, Suite 201, St. Paul, MN 55108, (612) 649-5750.

Pollution Control Agency, 520 Lafayette Rd., St. Paul, MN 55155, (612) 296-6300.

MISSISSIPPI • *Department of Environmental Quality*, Office of Pollution Control, P.O. Box 10385, Jackson, MS 39289-0385, (601) 961-5171.

MISSOURI • *Department of Natural Resources*, P.O. Box 176, Jefferson City, MO 65102, (314) 751-3176.

MONTANA • *Department of Health & Environmental Science*, Solid & Hazardous Waste Bureau, Cogswell Building, Helena, MT 59620, (406) 444-2821.

NEBRASKA • *Department of Environmental Control*, Litter Reduction & Recycling Program, P.O. Box 98922, State House Station, Lincoln, NE 68509-8922, (402) 471-2186.

NEVADA • *Office of Community Services*, Energy Extension Services, Capitol Complex, Carson City, NV 89710, (702) 687-4908.

New York City workers discard an estimated 600-700 tons of paper every day.

NEW HAMPSHIRE • *Environmental Services Department*, Waste Management Division, 6 Hazen Dr., Concord, NH 03301-6509, (603) 271-2926.

NEW JERSEY • *Department of Environmental Protection*, Office of Recycling, 850 Bear Tavern Rd., Trenton, NJ 08625-0414, (609) 530-4001.

NEW MEXICO • *Environmental Improvement Division*, Solid Waste Bureau, Harold Runnels Building, 1190 St. Francis Drive, Santa Fe, NM 87503, (505) 827-2959.

NEW YORK • *Department of Environmental Conservation*, Waste Reduction & Recycling, 50 Wolf Rd., Albany, NY 12233-4015, (518) 457-7337.

NORTH CAROLINA • *Solid Waste Section*, P.O. Box 27687, Raleigh, NC 27611-7687, (919) 733-0692.

NORTH DAKOTA • *Department of Health*, Division of Waste Management, P.O. Box 5520, Bismark, ND 58502-5520, (701) 224-2366.

OHIO • *Litter Prevention & Recycling*, Department of Natural Resources, 1889 Fountain Square, Building F-2, Columbus, OH 43224, (614) 265-6353.

OKLAHOMA • *Department of Health*, Solid Waste Services, P.O. Box 53551, Oklahoma City, OK 73152, (405) 271-7169.

OREGON • *Department of Environmental Quality*, Waste Reduction Section, 811 S.W. Sixth Ave., 8th Floor, Portland, OR 97204, (503) 229-5913.

PENNSYLVANIA • *Department of Environmental Resources*, Bureau of Waste Management, Waste Reduction/Recycling, P.O. Box 2063, Harrisburg, PA 17105-2063, (717) 787-7382.

RHODE ISLAND • *Department of Environmental Management*, O.S.C.A.R., 83 Park St., 5th Floor, Providence, RI 02903, (401) 277-3434.

The state of Maryland has been buying recycled paper since 1977.

SOUTH CAROLINA • *Bureau of Solid & Hazardous Waste*, 2600 Bull St., Columbia, SC 29201, (803) 734-5200.

SOUTH DAKOTA • *Department of Water & Natural Resources*, Waste Management Program, 523 E. Capitol St., Pierre, SD 57501, (605) 773-3153.

TENNESSEE • *Department of Health & Environment*, Solid Waste Management Division, 701 Broadway, 4th Floor, Customs House, Nashville, TN 37247-3530, (615) 741-3424.

TEXAS • *Department of Health*, Division of Solid Waste Management, 1100 W. 49th St., Austin, TX 78756, (512) 458-7271.

UTAH • *Department of Environmental Health*, Solid and Hazardous Waste, P.O. Box 16690, Salt Lake City, UT 84116-0690, (801) 538-6170.

VERMONT • *Department of Environmental Conservation*, Solid Waste Division, 103 S. Main St.,West Building, Waterbury, VT 05676, (802) 244-7831.

VIRGINIA • *Department of Waste Management*, 11th Floor, The Monroe Building, 101 N. 14th St., Richmond, VA 23219, (804) 225-2667, Hotline: (800) 552-2075.

WASHINGTON • *Department of Ecology*, Recycling Information Office, Eikenberry Building, 4407 Woodview Dr. S.E., Lacey, WA 98503, (206) 459-6731, Hotline: (800) RECYCLE.

WEST VIRGINIA • *Division of Natural Resources*, Solid Waste Section, 1356 Hansford St., Charleston, WV 25301, (304) 348-5993.

WISCONSIN • *Department of Natural Resources*, Bureau of Solid & Hazardous Waste Management, P.O. Box 7921, Madison, WI 53707, (608) 267-7566.

WYOMING • *Department of Environmental Quality*, Solid Waste Management, 122 W. 25th St., Herschler Bldg., 4th Floor West, Cheyenne, WY 82002, (307) 777-7752.

In Asian paper mills, computer paper is sometimes used as a substitute for virgin paper pulp.

STATE RECYCLING ASSOCIATIONS

These groups have been assembled by professional recyclers to serve their communities with practical information about recycling and recycling legislation. They're among the best sources of data on recycling in your area, and their brochures are usually pretty good. Note: They're privately-run organizations, so they may only have part-time staffs.

CALIFORNIA • *California Resource Recovery Association*, 13223 Black Mountain Rd., I-300, San Diego, CA 92129.

Northern California Recycling Association, P.O. Box 5581, Berkeley, CA 94705.

CONNECTICUT • *Connecticut Recyclers Coalition*, P.O. Box 445, Stonington, CT 06378.

FLORIDA • *Recycle Florida*, c/o Department of Environmental Regulation, Solid Waste Division, 2600 Blairstone Rd., Tallahassee, FL 32301.

HAWAII • *Recycling Association of Hawaii*, 162-B North King St., Honolulu, HI 96817, (808) 599-1976.

ILLINOIS • *Illinois Recycling Association*, 407 S. Dearborn #1775, Chicago, IL 60637, (312) 939-2985.

INDIANA • *Indiana Recycling Coalition*, P.O. Box 6357, Lafayette, IN 47903.

IOWA • *Iowa Recycling Associaton*, P.O. Box 3184, Des Moines, IA 50316.

KENTUCKY • *Kentucky Recycling Association*, c/o Urban County Government, Department of Public Works, 200 E. Main, Lexington, KY 40507.

The average American throws out 2 lbs. of plastic containers every month.

MAINE • *Maine Resource & Recovery Association*, c/o Maine Municipal Association, Community Dr., Augusta, ME 04330.

MARYLAND • *Maryland Recycling Coalition*, 101 Monroe, 6th Floor, Rockville, MD 20850.

MASSACHUSETTS • *MassRecycle*, P.O. Box 3111, Worcester, MA 01613.

MICHIGAN • *Michigan Recycling Coalition*, P.O. Box 10240, Lansing, MI 48901.

MINNESOTA • *Recycling Association of Minnesota*, c/o The Minnesota Project, 2222 Elm St. S.E., Minneapolis, MN 55414, (612) 378-2142.

MISSOURI • *Missouri State Recycling Association*, P.O. Box 331, St. Charles, MO 63301.

MONTANA • *Associated Recyclers of Montana*, 458 Charles, Billings, MT 59101.

Keep Montana Clean and Beautiful, P.O. Box 5925, 2021 11th Ave., Helena, MT 59601, (406) 443-6242.

NEBRASKA • *Nebraska State Recycling Association*, P.O. Box 80729, Lincoln, NE 68501, (402) 475-3637.

NEVADA • *Nevada Recycling Coalition*, 2550 Thomas Jefferson, Reno, NV 89509.

NEW HAMPSHIRE • *New Hampshire Resource Recovery Association*, P.O. Box 721, Concord, NH 03301-0721, (603) 224-6996.

NEW JERSEY • *Assoc. of New Jersey Recyclers*, 120 Finderne, Bridgewater, NJ 08807, (201) 722-7575.

NEW MEXICO • *Recycle New Mexico*, c/o Office of Recycling, City of Albuquerque, P.O. Box 1293, Albuquerque, NM 87103, (505) 761-8176.

Don't recycle tea bags with paper—compost them instead.

NEW YORK • *New York State Association for Recycling*, 1152 County Rd. #8, Farmington, NY 14425.

NORTH CAROLINA • *North Carolina Recycling Association*, P.O. Box 25368, Raleigh, NC 27611-5368, (919) 782-8933.

NORTH DAKOTA • *North Dakota Recyclers Association*, c/o Sam McQuade, P.O. Box 1196, Bismarck, ND 58502-1196

OHIO • *Association of Ohio Recyclers*, 200 S. Green St., Georgetown, OH 45121.

OREGON • *Association of Oregon Recyclers*, P.O. Box 15279, Portland, OR 97215, (503) 233-7770.

PENNSYLVANIA • Pennsylvania Resources Council, P.O. Box 88, Media, PA 19063, (215) 565-9131.

SOUTH CAROLINA • *Recycling Association*, c/o South Carolina Clean and Beautiful, 1205 Pendleton St., Room 203, Columbia, SC 29201, (803) 734-0143.

SOUTH DAKOTA • *Recycling Coalition of South Dakota*, 1800 Otonka Ridge, Sioux Falls, SD 57069.

TENNESSEE • *Tennessee Recycling Coalition*, 1725 Church St., Nashville, TN 37203.

TEXAS • *Recycling Coalition of Texas*, P.O. Box 2359, Austin, TX 78768.

VERMONT • *Association of Vermont Recyclers*, P.O. Box 1244, Montpelier, VT 05601, (802) 229-1833.

WASHINGTON • *Washington State Recycling Association*, 203 E. Fourth Ave. #307, Olympia, WA 98501, (206) 352-8737.

WISCONSIN • *Associated Recyclers of WI*, 16940 W. Shadow Dr., New Berlin, WI 53151, (414) 679-2132.

WYOMING • *Wyoming Citizens for Recycling*, P.O. Box 2393, Casper, WY 82602-2393.

The average American throws out about 6 lbs. of tin cans every month.

NATIONAL ORGANIZATIONS

These groups deal with recycling every day and know the practical details. Contact them if you want more information... or want to get more involved in the recycling movement.

Citizens Clearinghouse for Hazardous Wastes, P.O. Box 926, Arlington, VA 22216; (703) 276-7070. *Call if you're working on recycling legislation at the local level. Also has networking information.*

Coalition for Recyclable Waste, P.O. Box 1091, Absecon, NJ 08201; (619) 576-1996. *Targets products that aren't recyclable, stages protests and advises industries on alternatives. Send $15 to be on their "Action Alerts" mailing list.*

Earthworm, 186 South St., Boston, MA 02111; (617) 426-7344. *Hotline for finding and establishing recycling programs.*

Environmental Action, 1525 New Hampshire Ave. N.W., Washington, D.C. 20036, (202) 745-4870. *Extensive information on plastics, tires, toxics. Free listing of recycling contacts and publications.*

Environmental Defense Fund, 257 Park Ave. S., New York, NY 10010; (212) 505-2100. *Many excellent publications—for their free recycling brochure, dial (900) 454-3400.*

Inform, 381 Park Ave. S., Suite 1201, New York, NY 10016; (212) 689-4040. *Free fact sheets on garbage and recycling.*

Institute for Local Self-Reliance, 2425 18th St. N.W., Washington, D.C. 20009; (202) 232-4108. *Helps cities and community developers make new products from recycled materials.*

Institute of Scrap Recycling Industries, 1627 K St. N.W. Suite 700, Washington, D.C. 20006, (202) 466-4050. *Represents scrap processors and brokers. Brochures on metals, paper.*

Oregon passed the first U.S. bottle bill in 1971.

Keep America Beautiful, 9 W. Broad St., Stamford, CT 06902, (203) 323-8987. *Focuses on litter and recycling.*

Local Solutions to Global Pollution, 2121 Bonar St., Studio A, Berkeley, CA 94702, (415) 540-8843.

National Consumers League, 815 15th St. N.W., Suite 516, Washington, D.C. 20005, (202) 639-8140. *Tips on "smart shopping" and recycling.*

National Recycling Coalition, 1101 30th St. N.W., Suite 305, Washington, D.C. 20007, (202) 625-6406. *Sponsors the largest annual conference on recycling.*

Natural Resources Defense Council, 40 W. 20th St., New York, NY 10011, (212) 727-2700. *Ask for their guide to garbage.*

Plastics Recycling Foundation, 1275 K St. N.W., Suite 400, Washington, D.C. 20005, (202) 371-5212. *Sponsors research on plastic recycling.*

Renew America, 1400 16th St. N.W., Suite 700, Washington, D.C. 20036, (202) 232-2252. *Provides examples of successful recycling programs.*

SWICH, P.O. Box 7219, Silver Spring, MD 20901, (800) 67-SWICH. *EPA-funded information clearinghouse; provides guides, reports and pamphlets on recycling.*

World Resources Institute, 1709 New York Ave. N.W. Suite 700, Washington, D.C. 20006, (202) 638-6300. *Information on setting up a recycling program in the office.*

Most recycled PET comes from the 10 states with plastic container deposit laws.

PUBLICATIONS

MAGAZINES

Resource Recycling, P.O. Box 10540, Portland, OR 97210, (800) 227-1424, (503) 227-1319. *The ultimate source on recycling. Reports on projects throughout the U.S. and Canada; $42 per year.*

Garbage: The Practical Journal for the Environment, Old House Journal Corp., 435 Ninth St., Brooklyn, NY 11215, (718) 788-1700. *Colorful, interesting and fun to read; $21 per year.*

Biocycle: The Journal of Waste Recycling, The JG Press, Inc., P.O. Box 351, Emmaus, PA 18049, (215) 967-4135. *Monthly magazine that covers waste reduction and composting; $55 per year.*

E: The Environmental Magazine, P.O. Box 6667, Syracuse, NY 13217. (203) 854-5559. *Information about environmental issues for both the general public and seasoned environmentalists. $20.*

Recycling Today, Gie, Inc., 4012 Bridge Ave., Cleveland, OH 44113; (216) 961-4130. *Recycling programs, trend, $32 per year.*

Phoenix: Voice of the Scrap Recycling Industries, Institute of Scrap Recycling Industries, Inc., 1627 K St. N.W., Suite 700, Washington, D.C. 20006, (202) 466-4050. *Easy-reading industry magazine that covers recycling of metals, paper, glass and plastic. Free.*

Waste Age, National Solid Waste Management Association, 1730 Rhode Island Ave. N.W., Suite 1000, Washington, D.C. 20036, (202) 861-0708. *Covers solid waste issues and recycling; $45 per year. Also available:* **Waste Age's Recycling Times Newspaper.** *Covers recycling markets, $95/year.*

NEWSLETTERS

"All About Recycling," Pennsylvania Resources Council, P.O. Box 88, Media, PA 19063, (215) 565-9131. *Free with $30 membership.*

During World War I, reducing the weight of bicycles saved 2,000 tons of steel.

"Recycle!" Earth Care Paper Co., P.O. Box 14140, Madison, WI 53714-0140. (608) 277-2900. *An information booklet with the latest info on a variety of recycling issues, free.*

"Recycling World," Environmental Defense Fund, 257 Park Ave. S., New York, NY 10010, (212) 505-2100. *Tips on precycling, reports on community recycling, etc, send a self-addressed stamped envelope and 45¢.*

"The Sometimes Monthly Recycle Rag," Garbage Reincarnation, Inc., P.O. Box 1375, Santa Rosa, CA 95402. (707) 584-8666. *Covers local, state and national recycling issues, free.*

"Waste Watch," Californians Against Waste, 909 12th St., Suite 201, Sacramento, CA 95814, (916) 443-5422. *Legislative updates, free with a $20 membership.*

"Materials Recycling Markets," P.O. Box 577, Ogdensburg, NY 13669, (800) 267-0707. *Monthly newsletter covers northeastern U.S., Canadian recycling markets, $75 per year.*

"Warmer Bulletin," World Resources Foundation, 83 Mount Ephraim, Tunbridge Wells, Kent TN4 8BS, ENGLAND. *Great quarterly that covers world recycling issues, especially Europe's, free.*

"Wastelines," Environmental Action Foundation, 1525 New Hampshire Ave. N.W., Washington, D.C. 20036, (202) 745-4870. *Legislative updates on recycling around the country, $10 per year.*

REPORTS & GUIDES
"Mining Urban Wastes: The Potential for Recycling." *Excellent background, statistics on garbage and recycling, $4.*
and
"Packaging: Discarding the Throwaway Society." *A look at the effects of over-packaging. $4.* Both available from Worldwatch Institute, 1776 Massachusetts Ave. N.W., Washington, D.C. 20036, (202) 452-1999.

Recycling Works! EPA Office of Solid Waste, 401 M St. S.W., Suite 2817, Washington, D.C. 20460. *Details about state recycling programs, free. Call (800) 424-9346.*

Trees fertilized with Seattle sludge are reported to grow twice as fast as normal.

"Small Town and Rural Recycling Fact Packet," Environmental Action Foundation, 1525 New Hampshire Ave.N.W., Washington, D.C. 20036, (202) 745-4879. *A collection of articles on successful recycling programs, $5.*

Multi-Material Recycling Manual, Keep America Beautiful, 9 W. Broad St., Stamford, CT 06902, (203) 323-8987. *Comprehensive binder of information on a variety of materials, $55.50.*

Recycling: The Answer to Our Garbage Problems
Recycling program case studies, how to set up a program, $10.70.
and...
Solid Waste Action Guide Book
Discusses how to protest plans for a local incinerator, $8.98. Citizens Clearinghouse for Hazardous Wastes, Inc., P.O. Box 926, Arlington, VA 22216, (703) 276-7070.

Spreading the Word: A Publicity Handbook for Recycling, Association of New Jersey Environmental Commissions, P.O. Box 157, Mendham, NJ 07945, (201) 539-7547. *A how-to manual for promoting recycling programs, includes clip-art and repro sheets, $10.*

The Greenpeace Guide to Paper, Greenpeace Northwest, 4649 Sunnyside Ave. N., Seattle, WA 98103, (206) 632-4326. *A comprehensive guide that covers recycling, precycling and buying recycled products, $4.00 plus $1.50 for postage/handling.*

Waste: Choices for Communities, Concern, Inc., 1794 Columbia Road, NW, Washington, D.C. 20009. (202) 328-8160. *A 30-page guide, discusses the alternatives for dealing with garbage. $3.00.*

Why Waste A 2nd Chance: A Small Town Guide to Recycling, National Association of Towns and Townships, 1522 K St. N.W., Washington, D.C. 20005, (202) 737-5200. *Explains basic legislation, discusses recycling options for small communities, $11.50.*

American Recycling Market, Recoup, P.O. Box 577, Ogdensburg, NY 13669, (800) 267-0707. *A directory that lists 14,000 companies that buy recyclable materials, $95 (check the library).*

More than 60% of the waste collected on beaches is plastic.

BOOKS

Coming Full Circle: Successful Recycling Today, Environmental Defense Fund, 257 Park Ave. S., New York, NY 10010. (212) 505-2100. *Excellent overview of recycling in the U.S., $20.*

Beyond 40%: Record Setting Recycling and Composting Programs, Institute for Local Self-Reliance, 2425 18th St. N.W., Washington, D.C. 20009. (202) 232-4108. *Recycling case studies, $50($25 for non-profit and community groups).*

Complete Trash: The Best Way to Get Rid of Practically Everything Around the House, M. Evans and Company, Inc., 216 E. 49th St., New York, NY 10017, (212) 688-2810. *Tells how to dispose of everything from A-Z, $9.95.*

Facing America's Trash: What Next for Municipal Solid Waste? Government Printing Office, Superintendent of Documents, Washington, D.C. 20402, (202) 783-3238. *Good background reading, $16. Order # 052-003-01168-9.*

Garage Sale Mania! Betterway Publications, P.O. Box 219, Crozet, VA 22932, (804) 823-5661. *A guide to having a successful sale, $12.45. Also in bookstores.*

Recycling & Incineration: Evaluating the Choices. *Compares the economic and environmental effects of incineration versus recycling, $23.* Environmental Defense Fund, 257 Park Ave. S., New York, NY 10010; (212) 505-2100.
and
Rush to Burn: Solving America's Garbage Crisis? *Alternatives for averting a solid waste crisis, $17.95.* Island Press, P.O. Box 7, Covelo, CA 95428, (800) 828-1302.

OTHER MATERIALS

Recycling Wheel, Environmental Hazards Management Institute, P.O. Box 70, Durham, NH 03824, (800) 446-5256. *The fun way to get the basics on recycling: Just turn the wheel, $3.75.*

The Lone Recycler: A Comic Book on Recycling, Materials World Publishing, 1089 Curtis, Albany, CA 94706, (415) 524-8883. *A 40-page comic book for kids and adults, $4.15.*

Southwestern Bell hopes to recycle 2 million phone books in 1990.

MATERIALS INDEX